LEGEND

ed Books *showing the way*

OCAL STREET ATLAS

MILTON KEYNES

**BUCKINGHAM · DEANSHANGER · LEIGHTON BUZZARD
NEWPORT PAGNELL · WOBURN SANDS**

CONTENTS

≋≋≋	Pedestrianized / Restricted Access
═══	Track
⌐L	Built Up Area
-----	Footpath
∿	Stream
≋	River
≋Lock≋	Canal
━■━	Railway / Station
●	Post Office
P P+🚃	Car Park / Park & Ride
C	Public Convenience
✚	Place of Worship
→	One-way Street
i	Tourist Information Centre
▲8 ▲8	Adjoining Pages
▨	Area Depicting Enlarged Centre
▨	Emergency Services
▢	Industrial Buildings
▢	Leisure Buildings
▨	Education Buildings
▨	Hotels etc.
▨	Retail Buildings
▢	General Buildings
▨	Woodland
▨	Orchard
▢	Recreational / Parkland
▨	Cemetery

Every effort has been made to verify the accuracy of information in this book but the publishers cannot accept responsibility for expense or loss caused by an error or omission.

Information that will be of assistance to the user of the maps will be welcomed.

he representation on these maps of a road, track or path is no evidence of the existence of a right of way.

Street plans prepared and published by
Red Books (Estate Publications) Ltd, Bridewell House, Tenterden, Kent, TN30 6EP.
The Publishers acknowledge the co-operation of the local authorities of towns represented in this atlas.

 Ordnance Survey® This product includes mapping data licensed from Ordnance Survey® with the permission of the Controller of Her Majesty's Stationery Office.

www.redbooks-maps.co.uk

/O2007

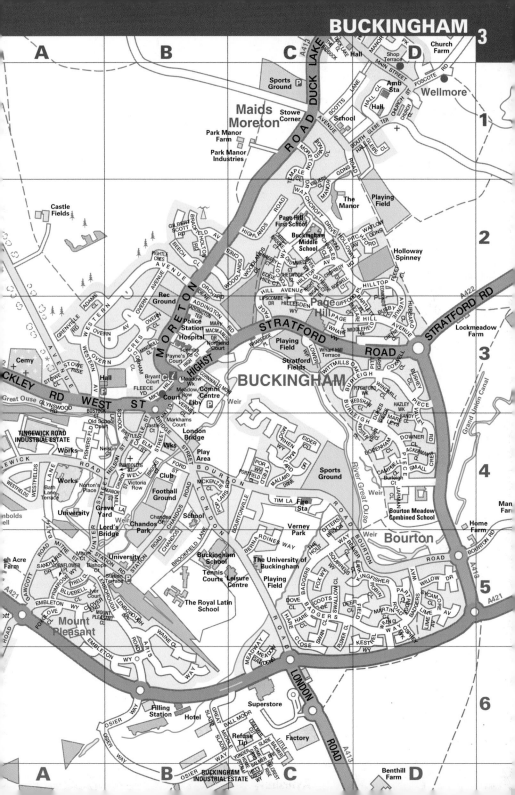

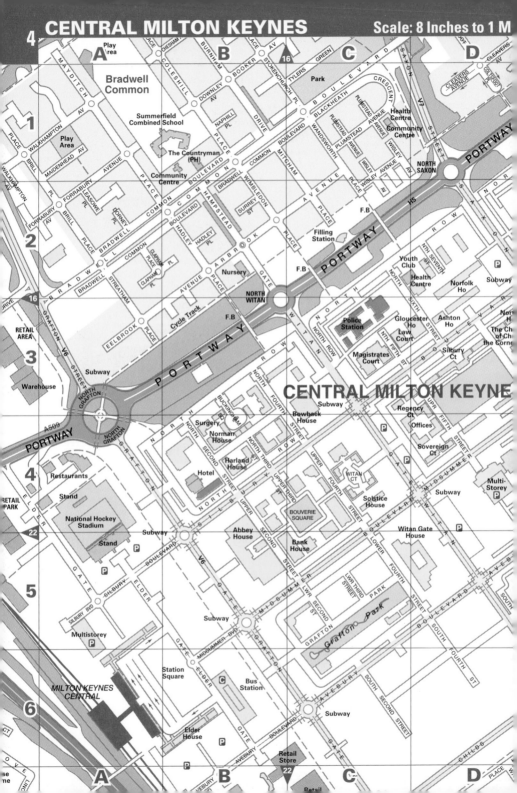

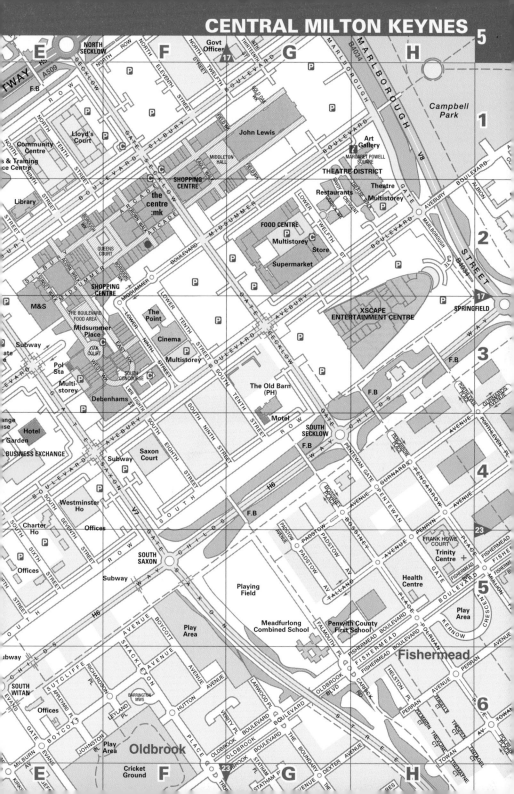

CENTRAL MILTON KEYNES

5

NORTH SECKLOW

Govt Offices

E **F** **G** **H**

Campbell Park

Community Centre

& Training ce Centre

Lloyd's Court

John Lewis

Art Gallery

MARGARET POWELL SQUARE

THEATRE DISTRICT

1

Library

the centre :mk

SHOPPING CENTRE

MIDDLETON HALL

Restaurants

Theatre

Multistorey

QUEENS COURT

FOOD CENTRE

Multistorey

Store

2

SHOPPING CENTRE

M&S

THE BOULEVARD FOOD AREA

The Point

Midsummer Place

OAK COURT

Cinema

Multistorey

Supermarket

XSCAPE ENTERTAINMENT CENTRE

SPRINGFIELD

17

Subway

Pol Sta

Multistorey

SOUTH CONCOURSE

Debenhams

The Old Barn (PH)

F.B

F.B

GUNNARDS AVENUE

3

Hotel Garden

BUSINESS EXCHANGE

Saxon Court

Motel

SOUTH SECKLOW

F.B

F.B

FRANK HOWE COURT

Subway

H6

F.B

Trinity Centre

4

Westminster Ho

Charter Ho

Offices

Offices

Subway

PENTEWAN GATE

Health Centre

FISHERMEAD

23

SOUTH SAXON

Subway

H6

Playing Field

Meadfurlong Combined School

Penwith County First School

Play Area

5

Offices

Play Area

Play Area

Fishermead

SOUTH WITAN

Offices

BARRINGTON MWS

Oldbrook

OLDBROOK BLVD

6

Cricket Ground

E **F** **G** **H**

23

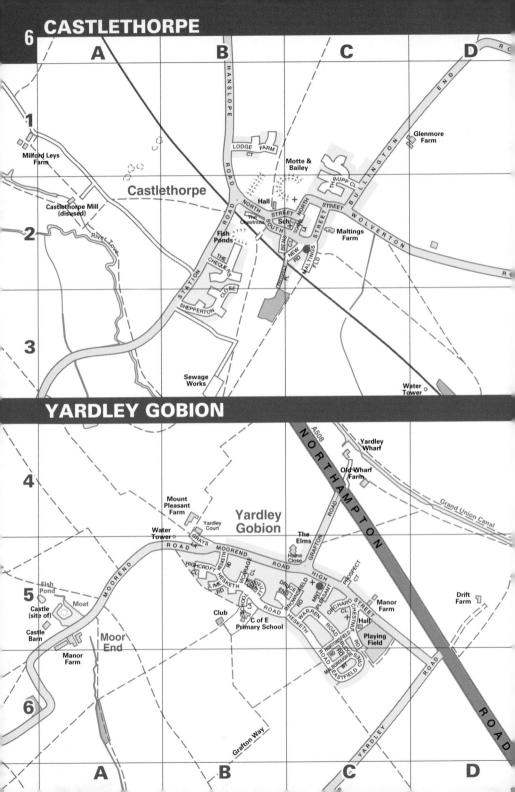

A   **B**   **C**   **D**

1

Milford Leys
Farm

LODGE CT

FARM

Motte &
Bailey

Glenmore
Farm

Castlethorpe

THRUPP CL

HANSLOPE ROAD

BULLINGTON END

2

Castlethorpe Mill
(disused)

River Tove

Hall

The
Chestnuts

Sch

NORTH STREET

SOUTH STREET

SOUTH LA

NORTH STREET

Maltings
Farm

WOLVERTON ROAD

Fish
Ponds

THE CHEQUERS

BENS CL

NEW RD

PRIORY PL

MALTINGS FLD

STATION ROAD

CLOSE

SHEPPERTON

3

Sewage
Works

Water
Tower

YARDLEY GOBION

4

A508

NORTHAMPTON

Yardley
Wharf

Old Wharf
Farm

Grand Union Canal

Mount
Pleasant
Farm

Yardley
Court

Yardley
Gobion

The
Elms

Water
Tower

GRAYS LA

MOOREND ROAD

HESKETH RD

Home
Close

GRAFTON ROAD

HIGH STREET

PROSPECT CT

5

Fish
Pond

Moat

Castle
(site of)

MOOREND ROAD

HIGHCROFT CL

LIME RD

HESKETH RD

SCHOOL LA

MORTAGE CL

WOODVILLE CRES

BROWNSFIELD END

DRUCES END

HESKETH RD

WARREN RD

MKT PLEASANT

ORCHARD CL

CHESTNUT RD

Manor
Farm

Drift
Farm

Castle
Barn

Club

C of E
Primary School

Hall

Playing
Field

**Moor
End**

Manor
Farm

HORTONSFIELD RD

EASTFIELD RD

MARLBOROUGH WY

YARDLEY ROAD

ROAD

6

Grafton Way

A   **B**   **C**   **D**

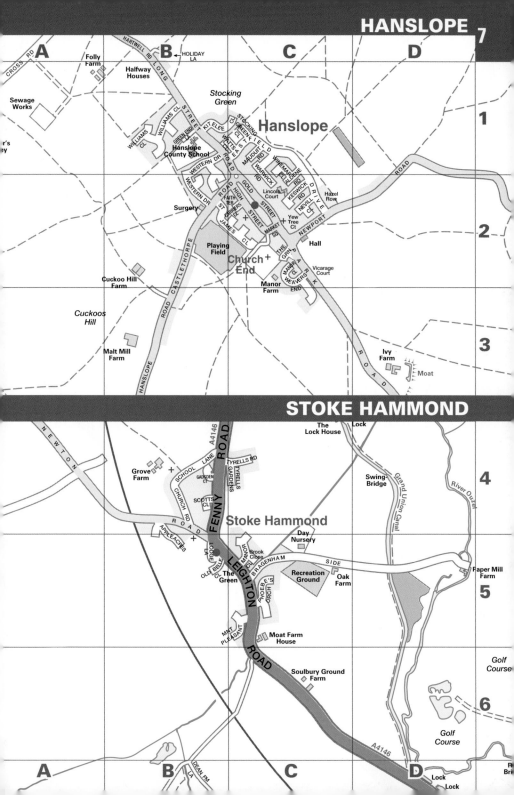

A B C D

CROSS RD
HARTWELL RD
HOLIDAY LA
Folly Farm
Halfway Houses
LONG STREET
Sewage Works
Stocking Green
WILLIAMS CL
r's ey
WILLIAMS CL
WESTERN DR
GREEN END ST
KITELEE CL
STOCKING FIELD
GREENFIELD CL
Hanslope
Hanslope County School
MAUDUIT RD
WARWICK RD
WINEMAR CL
ALDENE RD
Lincoln Court
KESWICK RD
NEVILL RD
Hazel Row
WESTERN DR
ROAD
HIGH STREET
GOLD STREET
FAITH GARDENS TER ST
Surgery
JAMES CL
Yew Tree Ct
MARKET SQ
NEWPORT ROAD
Playing Field
THE GRN
Hall
Church + End
MANN RD
WEAVERS END
PARK
Vicarage Court
Cuckoo Hill Farm
ROAD CASTLETHORPE
Manor Farm

Cuckoos Hill

Malt Mill Farm
HANSLOPE

ROAD
Ivy Farm
Moat

1
2
3

NEWTON
A4146 ROAD
The Lock House
Lock
Grove Farm
SCHOOL LANE
GADSDEN CT
TYRELLS RD
TYRELLS GARDENS
Swing-Bridge
Grand Union Canal
River Ouzel
CHURCH ROAD
SCOTTS CL
FENNY ROAD
Stoke Hammond
ROAD
APPLEACRES
OLD BELLE CL
LEIGHTON
BEDOOT CL
Brook Close
BRAGENHAM
Day Nursery
SIDE
The Green
PHOEBE'S ORCH
Recreation Ground
Oak Farm
Paper Mill Farm

MNT PLEASANT
Moat Farm House
ROAD
A4146
Soulbury Ground Farm

Golf Course

Golf Course

R Br
Lock
Lock

4
5
6

A B C D
DEAN FM LA

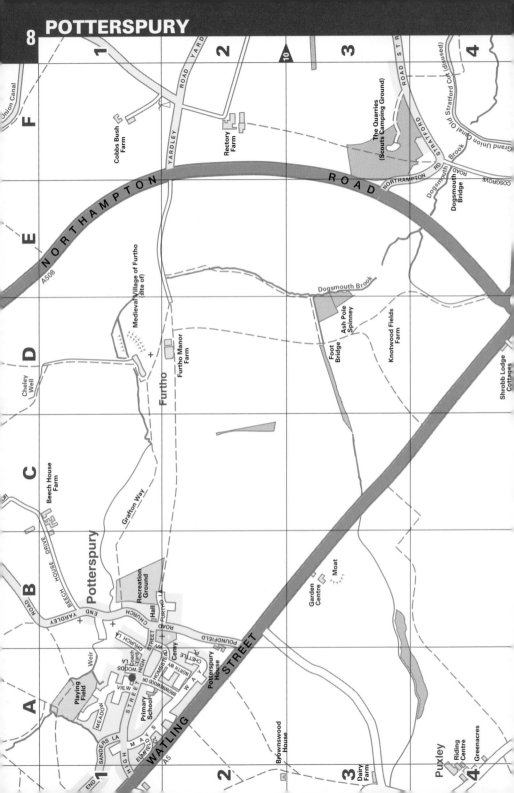

1

2

▲10

3

4

F

E

D

C

B

A

Cobbs Bush Farm

Rectory Farm

The Quarries (Scouts Camping Ground)

NORTHAMPTON ROAD

A508

ROAD

Dogsmouth Brook

Dogsmouth Bridge

COSGROVE ROAD

Old Stratford Cut (disused)

NORTHAMPTON RD

ROAD STR

Grand Union Canal

Union Canal

YARDLEY ROAD YARD

Medieval Village of Furtho (site of)

Cheley Well

Furtho

Furtho Manor Farm

Dogsmouth Brook

Foot Bridge

Ash Pole Spinney

Knotwood Fields Farm

Shrobb Lodge Cottages

Beech House Farm

Grafton Way

Potterspury

BEECH HOUSE DRIVE

YARDLEY END

ROAD

Recreation Ground

CHURCH END

Hall

CHURCH LA

STREET

Weir

Playing Field

MEADOW

HIGH STREET

VIEW

WOODS

Coach Yard

Cemy

HOMESTEAD

NORTH WAY

BROWNSWOOD DR

Primary School

SANDERS LA

MAY'S

ELMFIELD

HIGH END

WATLING STREET

A5

CASTLE PL

POUNDFIELD ROAD

FURTHO ROAD

Potterspury House

WATLING STREET

Garden Centre

Moat

Brownswood House

Dairy Farm

Puxley

Riding Centre

Greenacres

Net
Reserv

River Great Ouse

A5

5

5

CANALSIDE DRIVE

OXFIELD

WATER
Furtho
Court CL

COSGROVE

WHARF
LA

TRINITY
RD

PARK
DR

O

LONDON
ROAD

Hall

MOUNTHILL
AV

MOUNTHILL

WILLOW
AV

GR
GROVE

DICKENS CL

BROOKSIDE

HALL
DR

MANORFIELDS
RD

RIVERCREST
RD

HAWKWELL

Old Stratford

Primary
School

Comm
Centre

Play
Area

DEANSHANGER

QUEEN ELEANOR STREET

HIGH STREET

ROAD

FISONS RD

TEMPERANCE TER

10

Football
Field

St
Paul's
Court

Tennis
Court

Grove

MILL

STREET

HIGH STREET

CHURCH ST

York

YORK
LA

PROSPECT

Stratford
Arcade

OXFORD
ST

GOSEPARK

WILLOW
LA

HORN
LA

SILVER

6

7

Weir

Foot
Bridge

Foot
Bridge

River Great Ouse

20

Passenham

Manor
House

Manor
Farm

Pit

PASSENHAM

LANE

A422

8

F

E

D

ROAD

Chantry
Farm

Northfields

Shrob
Spinney

Buckingham Arm

Kingsbrook
School

Playing
Field

Tennis
Courts

Deanshanger

PUXLEY
ROAD

Spinney

Poultry
Farm

HAYES
ROAD

HAYES

FOXHOLES CL

GOOSEMERE

KINGSHILL
DR

HILL
DR

HONEY

DISWELL

BROOK

WINWOOD
CL

MOORS

NORTH
WY

PORTER'S CL

WAY

ROAD

WATFORD

HAYES

PATRICKS
LA

BUCKINGHAM

ROAD

THE GREEN

THE BEECHES

Primary
School
Playing
Fields

Scout
Hall

ROBERTS

WOODMANS

STREET

BDSWELL
LA

CHURCH LA

Dove
Court

Foot
Bridge

SPRINGFIELD GDNS

LITTLE LONDON

HIGH

Liby

ROAD

RIDGMONT

RIDGMONT

RIDGMONT
RISE

THE
RIDINGS

ELM DR

PUXLEY
ROAD

WESTFIELD

FOLLY

Playing
Field

GLEBE
ROAD

GLEBE
ROAD

HIGH
VIEW

HIGH VIEW

NORTH VIEW

AVENUE

ELM DR

Hanger
Lodge

Stollage
Lodge

Foot
Bridge

pinney

C

B

A

5

6

7

8

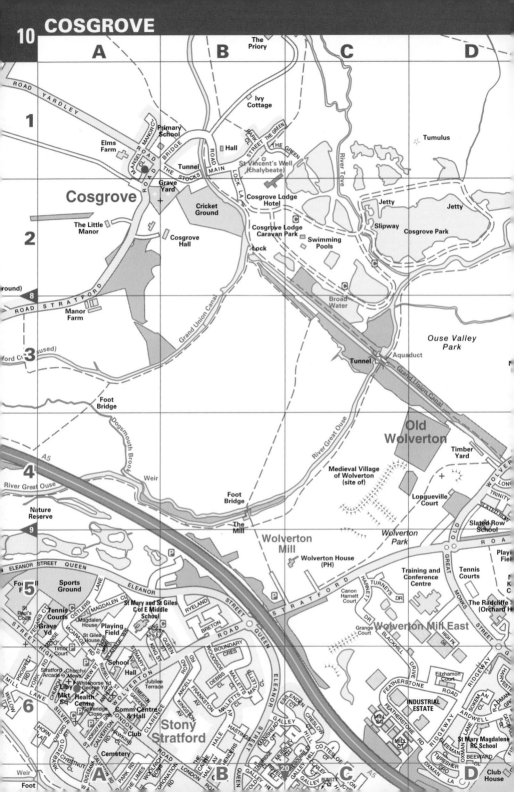

A   B   C   D

The Priory

ROAD YARDLEY

1

Elms Farm

MANSE ROAD
MANOR CL
THE STOCKS
BRIDGE ROAD

Primary School

Ivy Cottage

Hall

PARK CL
STREET
THE GREEN
THE GREEN

Tunnel

St Vincent's Well (chalybeate)

LOCK LA
MAIN ROAD

River Tove

Tumulus

Cosgrove

Grave Yard

The Little Manor

Cricket Ground

Cosgrove Hall

Cosgrove Lodge Hotel

Cosgrove Lodge Caravan Park

Lock

Swimming Pools

Jetty   Jetty

Slipway   Cosgrove Park

2

round)

ROAD STRATFORD

8

Manor Farm

Grand Union Canal

Broad Water

Ouse Valley Park

ford C(used)

3

Foot Bridge

Dogsmouth Brook

Tunnel   Aquaduct

Grand Union Canal

A5

4

Weir

River Great Ouse

Nature Reserve

River Great Ouse

Foot Bridge

Medieval Village of Wolverton (site of)

Longueville Court

Old Wolverton

Timber Yard

WOLVER
LON
TRINITY

SLATED ROW

Slated Row School

9

The Mill

Wolverton Mill

Wolverton Park

Wolverton House (PH)

Canon Harnett Court

Training and Conference Centre

Tennis Courts

The Radcliffe (Orchard H

ELEANOR STREET QUEEN

5

Fo
F

Sports Ground

ELEANOR

St Mary and St Giles C of E Middle School

RYELAND

STRATFORD
QUEEN

STRATFORD ROAD

Wolverton Mill East

TURNEYS DR
HARNETT
DR

BLACKHILL DRIVE

MONKS STREET

St Paul's Court

Tennis Courts

Grave Yd

Timbor Court

OSTLERS

MAGDALEN CL
WCARAGE RD

Magdalen House

St Giles House

Playing Field

KING CL
WINGS CL
WINGS CL

BRETON

WOODSIDE
BOUNDARY CRES

Grange Court

Fitzhamon Court

FEATHERSTONE ROAD

RIDGEWAY

HIGH PK

6

STREET HIGH
MILL
WILLOW LANE
PROSPECT RD
YORK RD
SILVER ST
OUSEBANK
CHESTNUT CL
HORN

School Hall

Stratford Arcade
Church
Mews
Whitehorse Yd
George Yd
Mkt Sq
Health Centre
Golfenide Close
Comm Centre & Hall
Club

Jubilee Terrace

Stony Stratford

Cemetery

RUSSELL ST
NEWS ST
WOLVERTON ROAD
GARRISON
LONDON RD
CALVERTON RD
HAWKINS
PARK RD
THE LIMES
WOOLLGAR
CORONATION RD

KINGSTON AV
CLARENCE RD

ANCELL
DEBBS CL
FRANKSTON AV

MALLETS CL
MILLETTS AV

HASTINGS RD
HALE
HENDERS

MANSHEAD CL
GALLEY
CRESLOW
HILL
COTTESLOE
GALLEY
MUDSLEY
RD

INDUSTRIAL ESTATE

FEATHERSTONE
MILL CT
MILL CT

FEEMANS
ARDWELL
LANE
THRESHER CL
BEEWARD

OXMAN LANE

St Mary Magdalene RC School

Weir

Foot

A   B   C   D

A5

Club House

20

E   F   G   Crossroads
Farm   H

Foot
Bridge

Haversham

1

Haversham County
Primary School

CHALMERS AV
ROWAN DR
KEPPEL AV
BROOKFIELD

WOLVERTON ROAD
MANOR DR
THE CRES
BEECH TREE CL

Haversham
Manor

Haversham County
Primary School

Fish
Ponds

Old R

River Great Ouse

2

Viaduct

HAVERSHAM ROAD

River Great Ouse

12

Recycling
Plant

Depot

COLTS   HOLM   ROAD

INDUSTRIAL
ESTATE

Works

Scrap
Yard

Depot

3

River Great Ou

COLTS HOLM RD
DICKENS
COLTS HOLM RD
OLD   WOLVERTON   ROAD
CANONS
DEAN'S
BRIDGETURN AV

Sports
Ground

Shed

Hall

GRAFTON STREET

WOLVERTON ROAD

Rec Grnd

New Brad

Club

Arden
Park

WATERSIDE
PARK

Factory

Factory

Works

Works

Depot

Wolverton
Park

Warehouse

WOLVERTON

NEWPORT

Grand Union Canal

Warehouse

Superstore

Comm
Centre

Training
Centre

STRATFORD ROAD

MCCONNELL DR

Stonebridge

NEWPORT ROAD

CALEDONIAN RD
WALLACE ST
WOOD ST
QUEEN ANNE ST
ST MARY ST
ST JAMES ST
ST GILES ST
KING EDWARD ST
QUEEN ANNE ST

HIGH

Club

New Bradwell
Combined School

4

Works

Works

Works

Works

RADCLIFFE ROAD

Club
Libry

Surgery

Hall
Hotel

Agora
Centre

City
Square

CAMBRIDGE ST
CHURCH ST
BUCKINGHAM

ST GEORGES ST

ST DAVIDS RD

Warehouse

FINGLE DR   FINGLE

GRAFTON

Aquaduct

STREET

16

STRATFORD ROAD
ORIEL CL
ORIEL CL
CHRISTCHURCH CL

Pol
Sta

Depot

Warehouse

ANSON ROAD
JERSEY ROAD
WINDSOR
Wyvern
School
AYLESBURY ST
PEEL ROAD

OXFORD ST
BEDFORD ST
THE BEDFORD ST
STACEY AV
VICTORIA STREET
OSBORNE STREET
MOUNT PLEASANT
LANE

Orchard
House

Bushfield Middle
School

Tennis
Courts

MCCONNELL DR

Warehouse

Blue
Bridge

BLACKWOOD CRES
VANDER BY
VICT
CULBERTSON
WEINA GRO
GARDINER CT
CONSTANTINE LANE
MORTON FORK
LANE
WAY

5

HALTONCHES

Radcliffe
School
(organ Hall)

Club

Swimming
Pool

Recreation
Ground

ETON CRES
AYLESBURY STREET   WEST
WOBURN AV
FURZE   WAY
WINDSOR STREET
WESTERN ROAD

Club

Cricket
Ground

MARINA DRIVE

Recreation
Ground

Club

AVENUE

Club

Blue
Bridge

SPOONLEY DR
WILLINGSTONE DR

MILLERS
WOODY
Club

GREATCHES
CHESTERHOLM

6

Cemetery

Wolverton

FRANK ATTER WAY
MARRON STREET
Goddard
Croft

Play
Area

Horners
Croft

Museum

DRIVE

WHITE BANK
BUCKTHORN
ALDER

Bancroft

Weir

Greenleys
County Middle
School

Wolverton Health Centre
& Day Hospital

ST JOHN'S CRES
WOODLAND VIEW
GLOUCESTER
FRANKLINS
GREAT MONKS STREET
LANE

SOUTHERN

MILLERS WAY
MYRTLE
BRIAR HILL
PLUM
ALDER

WILLOWFORD

KENCHESTER
OCTAVIA
HADRIAN

MONKS
BUCKMAN CL
CALDWELL CL
HERDMAN CL
PLOWMAN CL
TELLMAN CL

Greenleys
First School

Calvards
Croft

Barkers
Croft

Lamberts
Croft

E   F   21
Comm   Brian
Lodden   G   H

A   **B**   **C**   **D**

Midshires Way
Swans Way

The Cob

The Spinney

Little Linford

Dovecote Spinney

Linford Hall

Hall Farm

Duckpond Spinney

Linford Court

Bury Court

The Wilderness

1

The Serpentine

Little Linford Park

2

Reservoir (cover

Club

LINL

Parc Farm

Hill Farm

3

Haversham Mill

Bridge

Weir

River Great Ouse

River Great Ouse

Sailing Club

4

Linford Lakes

The Old Rectory

Wildfowl Study Centre

Marble Inn

11

St Peters (rems)

Hanslope Circular Ride

sh nds

5

Grand Union Canal

Stantonbury Wharf

Stantonbury Park Farm

Offices

P

6

Gravel Pit

CHURCHLEES

SANDY CL

ST LEGER

ANNES GRO

BUTLERS

River Great Ouse

Civic Amenity Site

Cemy

STREET

MARLBOROUGH

ASHFIELD

CROSSLAN

KEATS

WOLVERTON

BROAD

GRO

MARLBOROUGH

SPENCER

MELTON

ASHFIELD

16

A   **B**   **C**   **D**

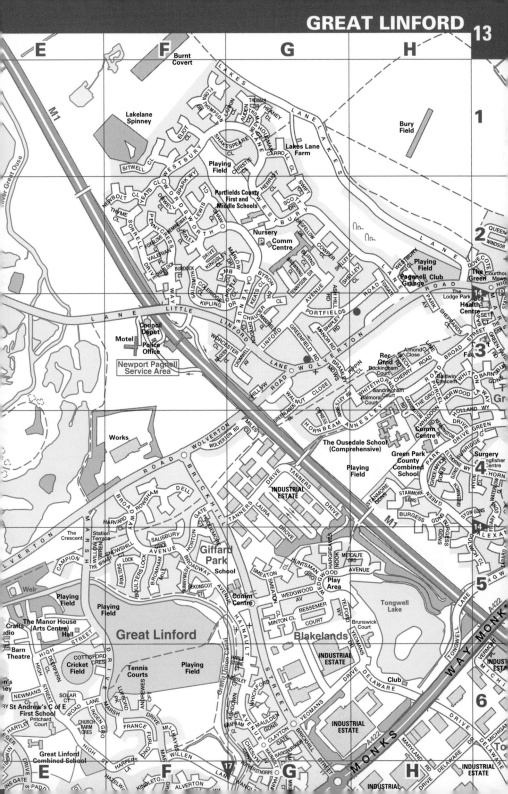

E F G H

1

M1

Burnt Covert

Lakelane Spinney

Lakes Lane Farm

Lakes Lane

Bury Field

Thomas Hearney Cl

Playing Field

Portfields County First and Middle Schools

Lakes Lane Farm

QUEEN

WINDSOR

2

Nursery

Comm Centre

Westbury

Playing Field

Pagenell Club

Pagenell Grange

The Green

The Courthouse Mews

HIG

14

Council Depot

Police Office

Motel

Newport Pagnell Service Area

Portfields

The Lodge Park

Health Centre

SSET

14

3

Rec Gnd

Buckingham Court

Almond Cl

Cherry

Baldwin Crescent

Sandringham Court

Balmoral Court

Whitethorn

Fa

Gr

Works

Wolverton Rd

Wolverton Road

The Ousedale School (Comprehensive)

Playing Field

Green Park County Combined School

Comm Centre

Surgery

Kingfisher Centre

HORN

4

14

INDUSTRIAL ESTATE

Tanners Drive

Laura Drive

BURGESS

Broad Way

Rowsham

Dell

Brick Hill

Tanners Drive

Harvard

Station Terrace

Salisbury Avenue

Snowshill

Broadway

Giffard Park School

Smeaton

Huntsman Gro

Metcalfe Gro

Play Area

Avenue

5

The Crescent

Weir

Playing Field

The Manor House (Arts Centre)

Hall

Barn Theatre

Great Linford

Comm Centre

Wedgwood Av

Minton Cl

Bessemer Court

Telford

Brunswick Court

Tongwell Lake

Blakelands

Club

M1

MONKS WAY

A422

MONK

Crafts Studio

Great Linford

Cottisford Cres

Cricket Field

Tennis Courts

Playing Field

Harlestone

INDUSTRIAL ESTATE

YEOMANS

St Andrew's C of E First School

Newmans

Solar

Woad

Church Farm Cres

France

Willen

INDUSTRIAL ESTATE

6

Great Linford Combined School

Harpers La

Hazelwood

Kingleton

Alverton

17

Clayton Gate

Brickhill Street

Rainsborough

Maryland

INDUSTRIAL ESTATE

E F G H

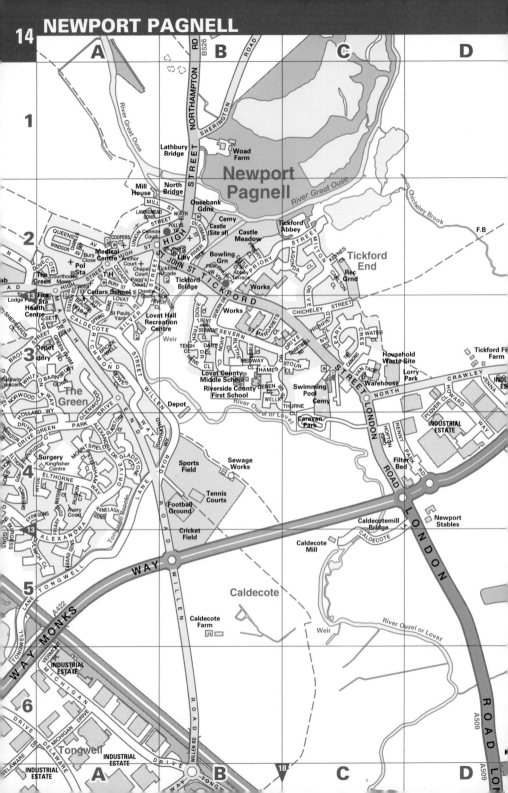

Newport Pagnell

A B C D

1

B526
NORTHAMPTON RD
ROAD
SHERINGTON
River Great Ouse
Lathbury Bridge
Mill House
North Bridge
Woad Farm
River Great Ouse
Chicheley Brook
F.B

2

QUEENSWAY
WINDSOR AV
CHARLES AV
DOVECOTE
The Green
Pol Sta
Medical Centre
Courthouse Mews
Cedars School
HIGH
CROSS ST
BURY ST
STATION RD
ST
LAWNSMEAD GDNS
NORTH SQ
COOPERS CT
HIGH
Anchor Court
Chapel Court
UNION
Cannon Court
POLLYS YD
ST JOHN'S ST
Tickford Arcade
Pagg's La
Chandos Ct
WATERSIDE
RIVER CL
NORTH ST
OUSEBANK
Ousebank Gdns
Cemy
Bowling Grn
PARK RD
Abbey Terrace
Tickford Bridge
HIGH ST
JOHN ST
TICKFORD
Liby
Castle Meadow
Castle (Site of)
Cemy
Tickford Abbey
PRIORY
CHURCH
LAGONDA
MILTON
KEYNES
CARLTON CL
Rec Grnd
STREET
Tickford End
Works
Works

3

SHEPHERDS CL
BROUGHTON
Depot
ictory
The Green
NORWOOD LA
HOLLAND WY
LAKES LA
BROOK
CALDECOTE
RICHMOND
BARN
GDNS
GREEN
BRINDLEWELL
ROWES
DRIVE
STREET
SILVER
SETT
ST Pauls Yard
Lovat Hall Recreation Centre
Weir
SPRING
LOVAT
TRENT
RENT
DERWENT
TEIGH CL
DART CL
NENE CL
DOVE
SEVERN DR
BLYTHE
MEDWAY
AVON
THAMES CL
STOUR CL
ST MARGARETS
CHICHELEY
HIGHFIELD
DRIVE
CRES
CARTMEL
CHARTWELL RD
VAN TAGE
THE CANONS
LEARY
WATER LA
Household Waste Site
Lovat County Middle School
Riverside County First School
DEBEN CL
WELLS
THURNE
Swimming Pool
Cemy
CP
Warehouse
Lorry Park
Tickford Fi Farm
CRAWLEY
PLOVER CL
HOWARD
JENNA
INDU ES
INDUSTRIAL ESTATE

4

ELLTHORNE
GREENWAY
HYDE
HILARY
RUSKIN
SYON GDNS
Surgery
Kingfisher Centre
MOUNT
SHELDRA
PETERSHAM
GLENWOOD
PARK
ALEXANDRA DR
GLADSTONE
DRIVE
GLASTONBURY
Avery Court
RANELAGH GDNS
ELDON
WILLEN
RICHMOND
Depot
ROAD
Sports Field
Sewage Works
Tennis Courts
Football Ground
River Ouzel or Lovat
Caravan Park
Caldecotemill Bridge
Swimming Pool
Filter Bed
LONDON
ROAD
HOPTON GRO
RENNY PARK RD
CLOWARD WAY
Newport Stables
Caldecote Mill

13

SYON GDNS
BURGESS
MONKSWAY
ALEXANDRA
TABARD GDNS
TONGWELL
Cricket Field
CALDECOTE

5

WAY MONKS
A422
VERMONT
MICHIGAN
WAY
WILLEN
LANE
TONGWELL
Caldecote
Caldecote Farm
Weir
River Ouzel or Lovat
A509
ROAD
LONDON

6

DRIVE
DELAWARE
DE MICHIGAN DR
MICHIGAN DRIVE
INDUSTRIAL ESTATE
Tongwell
INDUSTRIAL ESTATE
INDUSTRIAL ESTATE
A509
LONDON

A B 18 C D A509

E · F · G · H

A509

Beech Spinney

Hill Farm

Chicheley Brook

1

ROAD NORTH CF

2

CRAWLEY

NORTH

3

Tickford Lodge Farm

4

Tickford Park Farm

5

Tickford Park

WOOD END LANE

6

NEWPORT ROAD CRANFIELD ROAD

WILLOW DR

Moulsoe

Compton Court

lsoe
ings

E · F · G · H

19

ROAD

Church

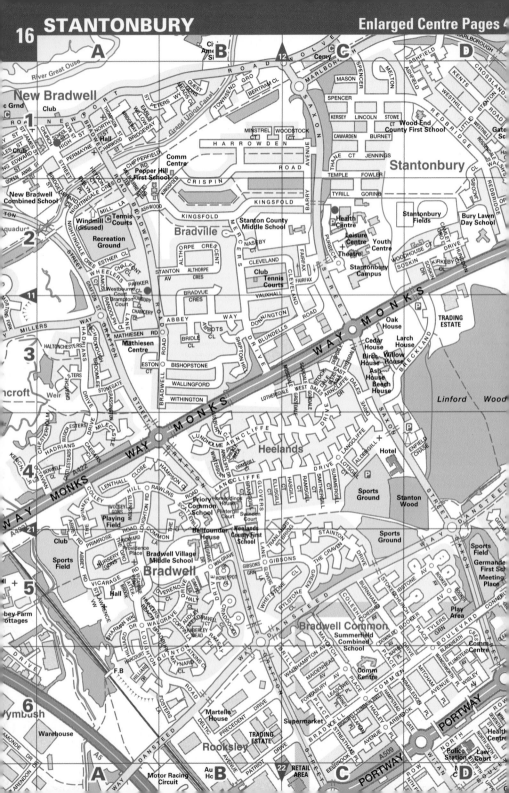

E   F ▲15   G   H

Compton
Court

NEWPORT ROAD

Church
Farm

1

Hermitage
Farm

2

M1

Old
Covert

3

Broughton
Barn

LONDON ROAD

Brooklands
Farm

New
Covert

4

AMBER
GATE

Hotel
BROUGHTON MANOR
BUSINESS PARK

Broughton

Ravenstone
House

BROUGHTON RD

5

LANE

BROUGHTON RD

NEWPORT ROAD

MILTON
OXREY
BULMER
HEDLEY
CREWS RAVENGLASS
SWANWICK

ESKDALE WY
RAVENSLASS CFT

GRIFFITH GATE

Surgery

S T R E E T

HALSWLL
WEBBS
WRENS PK
HOME

BRIDGE DIR
SWAYNE DRIVE
GREAT LINCH

A146

HIGHLEY DR
SWANWICK
LANE
KIDDERMINSTER WK

CHAFFRON WAY

DRIVE

WAY

Weir

Kingston
Bridge

NEWPORT ROAD

A5130

6

Fen
Farm

E   F   25   G   H

MAIDSTONE ROAD

Kingston

Stratford

A B C D

Weir
Foot Bridge

Cemetery

Cemy

St Mary Magdalene School

Club House

Rugby Foot Ground

1

Play Centre

Play Area

Watling Way County Middle & First School

Activities Centre

Play Area

Fullers Slade

Play Area

Play Area

Play Area

Play Area

WOOLMANS

MOORFOOT

SHEPHERDS

SIDLAW CT

MALVERN

BLACKDOWN

PENTLANDS

BELLWETHER

WEAVERS HILL

Rec Grnd

River Great Ouse

P

TUDOR GDNS

RIDGEWAY

QUEEN ELEANOR STREET

SLADE LANE

2

THORNTON

KILN FARM INDUSTRIAL ESTATE

Warehous

WATLING

CARTERS LA

PITFIELD

CARTERS

Quarry (dis)

Manor Farm

3

Calverton

Lower Weald

Middle Weald

4

Middle Weald Farm

Oakhill Lane Farm

5

Blacon Spinney

CALVERTON

Upper Weald

Weald Leys Farm

6

Middle Hill Farm

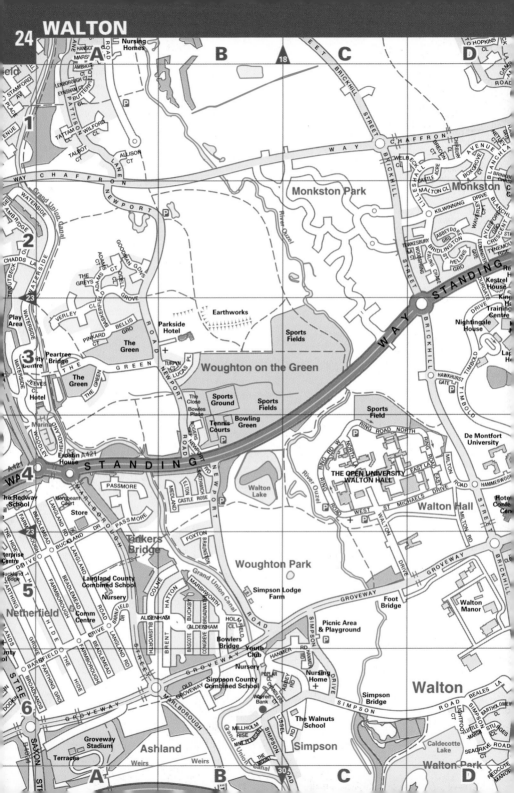

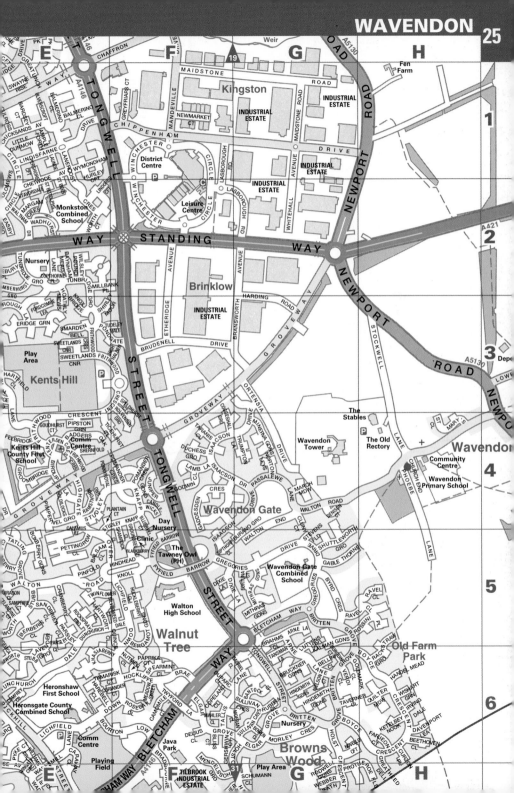

SHENLEY WOOD

Shenley Wood

Long Meadow School

Oxley Park Roundabout

Ash Pole Spinney

Shenley Wood

Medbourne

Reservoir

Earthworks

Playing Field

Hall

Grange Farm

Hazeley Wood

Oakhill Roundabout

H M PRISON WOODHILL

Oakhill Wood

Oakhill Wood

Oldland Covert

Shenley Dens Farm

Boundary Walk

Milton Keynes

Shenley Grounds Farm

Whaddon Common Farm

STRATFO

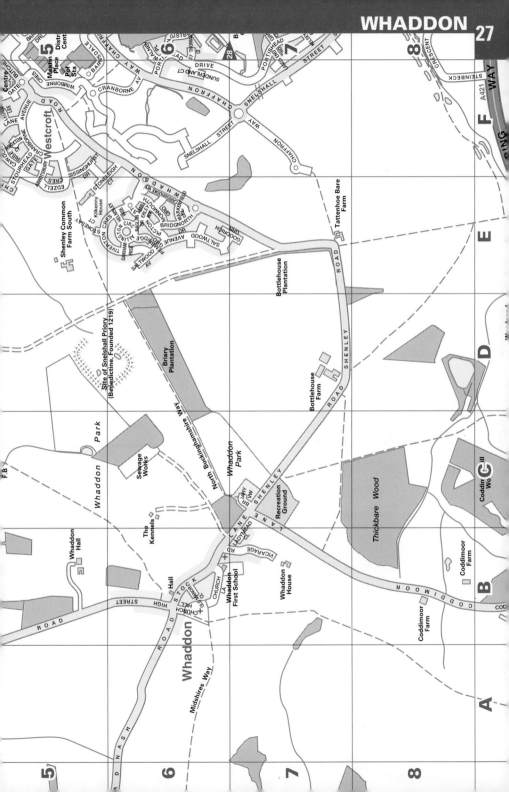

WHADDON

Westcroft

Shenley Common Farm South

Kilkenny House

Stoneleigh

Site of Snelshall Priory (Benedictine. Founded 1219)

Briary Plantation

Bottlehouse Plantation

Tattenhoe Bare Farm

Whaddon Park

Whaddon Park

Bottlehouse Farm

SHENLEY ROAD

Sewage Works

The Kennels

Recreation Ground

Thickbare Wood

Coddimoor Wood

Coddimoor Farm

Whaddon Hall

Whaddon First School

Whaddon House

Hall

Whaddon Hall

CHURCH

Coddimoor Farm

CODDIMOOR

Whaddon

Midshires Way

NASH ROAD

North Buckinghamshire Way

CHAFFRON WAY

SNELSHALL STREET

PORTISHEAD STREET

RING WAY

A421

STEINBECK CRESCENT

HIGH STREET

STOCK ROAD

CHURCH HILL

VICARAGE RD

LADYMEAD CLOSE

BRIARY WAY

SHENLEY LANE

District Cent

Pol Sta

Centre

WIMBORNE AVENUE

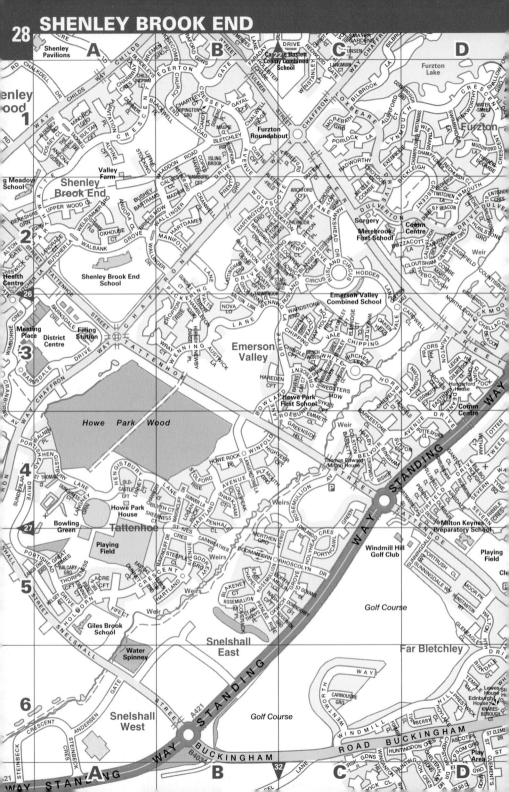

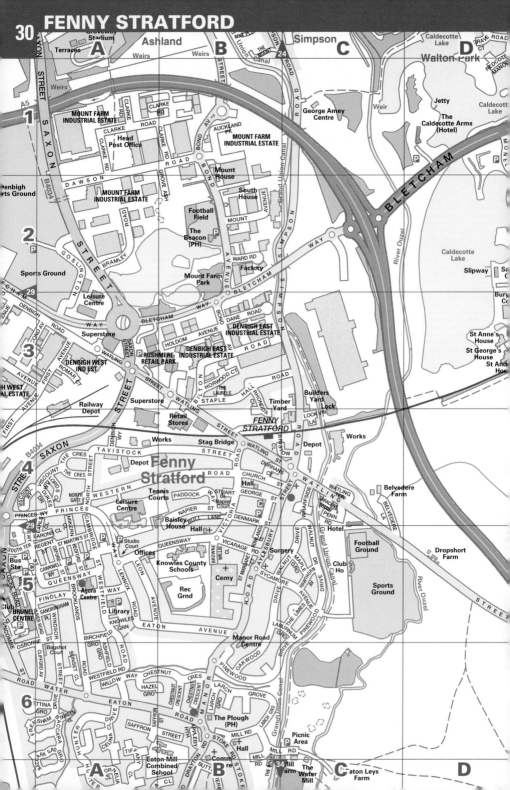

Groveway Stadium
Terraces
Ashland
Weirs
Weirs
Simpson
Caldecotte Lake
Walton Park
BRAVE ROAD CT
REDCOTE MANOR

A **B** **C** **D**

Union Canal
MNT
THE MOUNT
24

SAXON STREET
A5
B4034
Weirs

CLARKE RD
CLARKE ROAD
MOUNT FARM INDUSTRIAL ESTATE
Head Post Office
CLARKE RD
DAWSON

AUCKLAND PK
BOND AV
MOUNT FARM INDUSTRIAL ESTATE
Mount House
South House
George Amey Centre

Weir
Jetty
The Caldecotte Arms (Hotel)
Caldecotte Lake

1

Denbigh Sports Ground

MOUNT FARM INDUSTRIAL ESTATE
GROVE ASH
Football Field
The Beacon (PH)
ROAD
MOUNT
AVENUE
SIMPSON ROAD
BLETCHAM WAY
River Ouzel

BLETCHAM
MORE

Caldecotte Lake
Slipway

2
Sports Ground
GOSLINGTON
BRAMLEY
STREET
WARD RD
Factory
Mount Farm Park
BOND AVENUE
DANE ROAD
BLETCHAM WAY

Bury

CHAM
29
DENBIGH
COMMON AV
ROAD
Leisure Centre
W A Y   BLETCHAM
HOLDOM AVENUE
DENBIGH EAST INDUSTRIAL ESTATE

St Anne's House
St George's House
St And Hos

3
H WEST AL ESTATE
DENBIGH AV
FIRST AVENUE
Superstore
DENBIGH WEST IND EST
WATLING
SAXON STREET
RUSHMERE RETAIL PARK
DENBIGH EAST INDUSTRIAL ESTATE
ROAD
HALL STAPLE
THE LAURELS
HORWOOD CT
RHONDDA CT
Timber Yard
ROAD
Builders Yard
Lock
LOCK LA
LOCK VW

FIRST AVENUE
Railway Depot
Superstore
WATLING STREET
BILTON
FENNY STRATFORD
Depot
Works

B4034
SAXON
STREET
Works
TAVISTOCK
Stag Bridge
WATLING STREET
DURRANS
ST
WATLING

4
STRE
DENBIGH WY
THE CRES
THE CRES
VISCOUNT
Depot
Fenny Stratford
ROAD
Tennis Courts
PADDOCK
Hall
CHURCH ST
GEORGE ST
C
WHARFSIDE
Belvedere Farm
BELVEDERE LA

NORTH GATE
WESTERN
Leisure Centre
NAPIER ST
STUART ST
Napier Court
DENMARK ST
SARACENS
PENN
Hotel
Football Ground
Dropshort Farm

PRINCES WY
LORDS CL
DUKES
PRINCES
MINKEN
Baisley House
Hall
BULL LANE
VICTORIA
ST
 STREET
WALNUT
Club Ho
River Ouzel

5
Bus Sta
BARONS CL
CAMBRIDGE
REGENT
ST MARTIN'S ST
BEDFORD
Studio Court
Offices
QUEENSWAY
WILLIS
VICARAGE
ROWLANDS
AYLESBURY
Surgery
MAPLE
HAWTHORN DR
WALNUT DRIVE
Sports Ground
STREET

CAWKWELL ST
OXFORD
WAY
Knowles County Schools
BROWNE
MARGARET
SYCAMORE
LABURNUM GRO
PINEWOOD
29
Club
BRUNEL CENTRE
QUEENSWAY
FINDLAY
Agora Centre
LENNOX ROAD
Cemy
Rec Grnd
ROAD
THE LIMES

WYCOMBE ROAD
SANDRINGHAM
BROOKLANDS
Library
KNOWLES GRN
EATON
AVENUE
Manor Road Centre

OSBORNE ST
CLIFFORD AV
BIRCHFIELD
WESTFIELD
ASHFIELD
SUNSET CT
EATON
PINEWOOD
OAKWOOD

6
BETTINA GRO
FRENSHAM
BACCARA GRO
WATER
ROAD
WESTFIELD RD
CHESTNUT GRO
HAZEL GRO
WILLOW
CHESTNUT CRESCENT
CHESTNUT CRESCENT
LARCH
CRES
LARCH GRO
GROVE
MANOR ROAD
PINEWOOD
Picnic Area
Caton Leys Farm

HUNTER
CORNELIA
CLEVE
SAFFRON
TIFF ANY
The Plough (PH)
APPLEBY
DRAYTON
STOKE
Hall
STOKE RD
MILL RD
MILL RD
The Water Mill

Eaton Mill Combined School
Comm
34
Hill Farm

A **B** **C** **D**

STANDING WAY
BUCKINGHAM ROAD
B4034
28
STEINBECK CRES
WEASEL LANE
Milton Keynes Boundary Walk
THIRSK GDNS
WINCANTON HILL
HUNTINGDON CRES
CHEPSTOW DR
CHELTENHAM GDNS
ASCOT PL
EPSOM GRO
KELSO CL
HEXHAM GDNS
CLEMENTS DRIVE
HAYDOCK CL
KEMPTON GDNS
SANDOWN CT
CARTMEL CL
HAMILTON LA
AINTREE CL
FONTWELL DR
BLAYDON CL
NEWBURY CT
WETHERBY DRIVE
Play Area
Natural Gas Reception Centre
BLETCHLEY ROAD
Disused Railway
Recreation Ground
Hall
Manor Farm
Thick Thorn Farm
BERRY WAY
GREEN WAY
BONNARDS RD
BAY TREE CL
RED HOUSE CL
PARADISE
FIRE LA
CHURCH END
WHADDON ROAD
BETTY'S CL
LOWER END
MANOR RD
ST FAITH'S CL
Newton Longville
WESTBROOK END
COBB HALL RD
WARNERS RD
MOORFIELD
IVY LA
ORCHARD CL
LILAC CL
BROOKFIELD RD
YEW TREE CL
SCHOOL DR
Primary School
CROFTS LA
ELM CL
CHESTNUT CL
POND CL
BLETCHLEY
END
DRAYTON ROAD
DROVERS WY
Middle Salden Wood
Reservoir
Cowpasture Farm
Hounslow Hall
Brook Farm
Resevoir
NEWTON ROAD
A
B
C
D
1
2
3
4
5
6

E **F** **G** **H**

1

GE'S
ST PATRICK'S WAY
ST JOHN'S WAY
BEECHCROFT RD
ST DAVID'S RD
ST JOHN'S RD
St Matthews Court
ST ALBAN'S
WHITELEY
CRESCENT
WHITELEY CRES
NEWTON
CLOSE
NEWTON
ROAD
WHITELEY
ON GROVE

Red Grnd

Playing Field

Bowling Green

Sports Ground

29

Jetty

Landfill Site

Clay Pit

Brick Works

Blue Lagoon Park

P

BARTON

DRAYTON ROAD

Gar Clos

Cow Common Farm

2

Sports Ground

Landfill Site

Landfill Site

Landfill Site

New Covert

DOON WY
DRAYTON

34

3

Slad Farm

Slad Farm Cottage

4

Old Fox Covert

ROAD

STOKE

DRAYTON

34

5

Dead Queen Farm

Borough Farm

ROAD

NEWTON

Rectory Farm

6

Lady Villier's Gorse

ROAD

NEWTON

Common Farm

E **F** **G** **H**

E   F   G   H

A5
31

Broomhills Wood

1

Model Farm Cottages
Model Farm

The Clock House

WOBURN   RD

Playing Field

BRICKHILL MANOR CT

Park Spinnies

Little Brickhill

Community Centre

GREAT BRICKHILL LANE

WYNESS AV

Reservoirs (covered)

2

Field Close Plantation

A5

Brookfield Wood

Barden Pits

Battle Hills Farm

WATL

St Margarets Farm

Pipershill Spinney

3

Philip's Clump

Great Firs

Goodman's Wood

Duncombe Wood

Hanginglane Firs

4

The Moors

Lodgehill Wood

Fishpond Spinney

GALLEY   LANE

The Shrubberies

CHURCH   CL

Playing Field

Hall

Cemetery

Rectory Farm

LA   LOWER   ROTTEN   ROW

HOME FARM LA

Home Farm

5

Green End

High Ash C of E Combined School

Hillbottom Spinney

UPPER   AV

NAISBY DR

PENNYCUIK

HILL

Great Brickhill

POUND   CL

WITHERS   CL

KNIGHT   CL

WAY

HEATH   LANE

ROAD   HEATH   ROAD

Holt House Farm

6

The Green

STOKE   LANE

IVY   LANE

HOLTS GREEN

CUFF LANE

DUCK END

Stockgrove Farm

ROAD

E   F   G   H

Sewage Works

Foot

The Dower House

Baker's Wood

Stockgrove Country Park

Wood

Baker's Wood

Rushmere Park

Club

Sand Pit

St Leonard's Lower School

Rec Grnd

THRIFT ROAD

WOOD CL

BAKERS CL

REACH GREEN

Home Farm

BRICKHILL ROAD

Playing Field

Kennels

Kingswood Farm

Fox Corner

Sand Pit

Sand Pit

Sand Pit

OVEREN

Sand Pit

GRANGE GDNS

Red Lion Court

THOMAS ST

BIRD'S HILL

SHEEPCOTE CRES

THE DELL

Works

Weighbridge

Works

Conveyor

Heath and Reach

Club

Rushmere Park

Rushmere

LINSLADE ROAD

PLANTATION

Sewage Works

THE ABBEY WK

STILE

EMU CL

SYLVESTER ST

PINKLE HILL RD

LANE'S END

HEATH GDN

LANE'S END

Wellington House

Hall

REACH ROAD

GIG LANE

EASTERN

WAY

Clock Tower

Hall

Stables

Sandfield House

Spinney Court

Spinney Farm

LEIGHTON ROAD

Golf Course

Golf Course

Club House

THE HEATH CT
HEATH CL
HEATH CL
HEATH
DUKES RIDE
COURT

The Knolls

Oak Bank School

CRADDOCKS DR

SHENLEY

SHENLEY

ST LEONARD'S

HILL

ROAD

SHENLEY H

CARLTON GRO

OAK BANK

CHILTERN GDNS

THORNHILL WK

AVON WK

TAMAR WK

ISIS WK

SANDY LANE

HEATH

CUTTER WK

PARK ROAD

BEECH

CUTTER BEECH WY

HEATH PK DR

COTEFIELD DR

Heathwood Lower School

HEATHWOOD CL

THE WALNUTS

COTEFIELD DR

DRIVE

FIRS PATH

REDWOOD GLADE

Swiss Cottage (Nursing Home)

RIDE

TAYLOR'S RIDE

OXENDON CT

TAYLOR'S

RINGSWOOD LL

DINGLE DELL

WOODLAND

Grand Union Canal

Manor Court

Old Linslade Manor

River Ouzel

Dovery Down Lower School

CLOSE

PINE CL

THE

COTEFIELD

PINE CL

POPLAR

Broomhills Farm

Corbettshill Farm

Swing-bridge

Footbridge

HILLSIDE ROAD

ADAMS BOTTOM

Rec Grnd

CHAMBERLAINS GDNS

HEATH

GREENHILL

SHEPHERDS MEAD

Sand Pit

WOBURN SAND

Sand Pit

Factory

NELSON ROAD

VANDYK

Grand Union Canal

Leighton bk

ST

GLOB

CARNATION

BROOMHILL RD

HEATH ROAD

Spen Court

Vandy an

Youth

38

39

A - Z INDEX TO STREETS
with Postcodes

The Index includes some names for which there is insufficient space on the maps. These names are indicated by an * and are followed by the nearest adjoining thoroughfare.

Abbey Ho MK9   4 B4
Abbey Rd,
  Bradwell MK13   16 A4
Abbey Rd,
  Simpson MK6   14 C2
Abbey Ter MK16   14 B2
Abbey Walk LU7   37 C3
Abbey Way MK13   16 B3
Abbeydore Gro MK10   24 D2
Abbots Cl MK13   16 B3
Abbotsbury MK4   27 E5
Abbotsfield MK6   23 H2
Aberdeen Cl MK3   29 F2
Abraham Cl MK15   17 H2
Acacia Cl LU7   39 H3
Ackerman Cl MK18   3 D4
Acorn Walk MK9   5 E2
Adaern Cl LU7   39 E2
Adams Bottom LU7   37 C6
Adams Cl MK18   3 A3
Adams Ct MK6   24 A2
Adastral Av LU7   39 H4
Addington Rd MK18   3 B3
Addington Ter MK18   3 B3
Adelphi St MK9   17 F5
Ainsdale Cl MK3   28 D4
Aintree Cl MK3   32 C1
Akerman Cl MK12   11 E6
Akister Cl MK18   3 D4
Albany Cl MK14   16 D1
Albany Rd LU7   39 F3
Albert St MK2   29 H4
Albion Pl MK9   5 H2
Albury Ct MK8   21 H5
Aldenham MK6   24 A5
Aldergill MK13   16 C4
Aldermead MK12   21 G1
Alderney Pl MK15   18 B1
Aldrich Dr MK15   18 B1
Aldwycks Cl MK5   26 F1
Alexandra Ct LU7   38 D2
Alexandra Dr MK14   14 A4
All Saints Vw MK5   22 B2
Alladale Pl MK12   21 G1
Allen Cl MK2   34 A2
Allerford Ct MK4   28 C1
Allington Circle MK4   27 E6
Allison Ct MK15   24 A1
Almond Cl MK3   13 H3
Almond Rd LU7   39 G1
Alpha Ct LU7   39 F3
Alpine Cft MK5   28 A1
Alston Dr MK13   21 G2
Alstonefield MK4   28 B1
Althorpe Cres MK13   16 B2
Alton Gate MK4   26 F4
Alverton MK14   17 F1
Alwins Fld LU7   38 B1
Ambergate MK16   19 E4
Amberley Walk MK4   27 E6
Ambridge Gro MK6   23 H2
Ambrose Ct MK15   24 A1
Amelias La MK9   17 G6
Amos Ct MK13   16 A2
Ampleforth MK10   25 E1
Ancell Rd MK11   10 B6
Anchor Ct MK16   14 A2
Ancona Gdns MK5   28 A1
Andersen Gate MK4   28 A6
Andrewes Cft MK14   13 F6
Angel Cl MK15   17 F2
Angelica Ct MK7   25 E5
Anglesey Cl MK8   22 A2
Angora Cl MK5   28 A2
Angstrom Cl MK5   22 C5
Angus Dr MK3   29 F2
Annes Gro MK4   12 D6
Annesley Rd MK16   13 G4
Anson Rd MK12   11 E5
Anthony Ct MK11   10 A6
Appenine Way LU7   39 G2
Apple Tree Cl LU7   38 B3
Appleacres MK17   7 B4
Appleby Heath MK2   30 B6
Applecroft MK17   32 D3
Appleton Mews MK4   28 B2
Appleyard Pl MK6   5 E6
Aquila Rd LU7   39 H2
Arbroath Cl MK3   29 E2
Arbrook Av MK13   4 B2
Archers Wells MK3   29 G3
Archford Cft MK4   28 C2
Ardmore Cl MK10   19 E6
Ardwell La MK12   10 D6

Ardys Ct MK5   22 B2
Aries Ct LU7   39 G1
Aris Way MK18   3 B5
Arlington Cft MK4   29 E2
Arlott Cres MK6   23 F3
Armourer Dr MK14   17 F3
Armstrong Cl MK8   26 E1
Arncliffe Dr MK13   16 B4
Arne La MK7   25 G5
Arrow Pl MK2   34 B3
Arundel Gro MK3   29 E5
Ascot Dr LU7   38 B3
Ascot Pl MK3   28 D6
Ash Grange LU7   39 F4
Ash Gro LU7   39 E1
Ash Hill Rd MK16   13 G2
Ash Ho MK14   16 C3
Ashburnham Cl MK3   28 D4
Ashburnham Cres LU7   38 C4
Ashby MK6   23 G3
Ashby Ho MK6   23 G4
Ashdown Cl MK14   13 G6
Ashfield MK14   16 D1
Ashfield Gro MK2   30 A5
Ashford Cres MK8   26 D1
Ashlong Cl LU7   39 G3
Ashpole Furlong MK5   22 B4
Ashridge Cl MK3   28 D6
Ashton Ho MK9   4 D3
Ashwell St LU7   39 E2
Ashwood MK13   16 A2
Asplands Cl MK17   36 B3
Aspley Ct MK17   36 C3
Aspley Hill MK17   36 C3
Aspley La MK17   36 E4
Astlethorpe MK8   21 H4
Aston Cl MK5   22 B6
Atherstone Ct MK8   21 F3
Atkins Cl MK13   16 B6
Atterbrook MK13   16 A5
Atterbury Av LU7   39 F2
Attingham Hill MK8   22 A2
Atwell Cl MK8   26 E1
Auckland Pk MK1   30 B1
Auden Cl MK16   13 G1
Audley Mead MK13   16 B5
Augustus Rd MK11   20 A1
Aurora Ho MK13   22 B1
Austwick La MK4   28 B3
Avebury Blvd MK9   5 F4
Avebury Boulevard MK9   4 B6
Aveline Ct LU7   39 E3
Avenue Rd MK18   3 C1
Avery Cl LU7   39 G5
Avery Ct MK16   14 A4
Avington MK8   21 G5
Avon Cl MK16   14 B3
Avon Gro MK3   29 E5
Avon Walk LU7   37 D4
Aylesbury St,
  Milton Keynes MK2   30 B5
Aylesbury St,
  Wolverton MK12   11 F5
Aylesbury St West MK12   11 E5
Aylesford Gro MK10   24 D2
Aynho Ct MK8   21 H5
Ayr Way MK3   29 E2

Babington Cl MK10   19 E6
Baccara Gro MK2   30 A6
Back Wood MK17   31 G4
Backleys MK7   31 E2
Badgemore Cft MK4   21 F3
Badgers Oak MK7   25 E4
Badgers Way MK18   3 C5
Badminton Vw MK8   22 A2
Bagshot Ct MK16   30 A6
Baily Ct MK5   22 B6
Baisley Ho MK2   30 B4
Baker St LU7   39 E2
Bakers Wood Cl LU7   37 C1
Bala Cl MK2   34 A2
Bala Way MK2   34 A1
Balcary Gro MK4   28 A5
Baldwin Cres MK16   13 H3
Balfe Mews MK7   31 G1
Ball Moor MK18   3 B6
Balmer Cut MK18   3 C6
Balmerino Cl MK18   25 E1
Balmoral Cft MK16   13 H3
Balsam Cl MK7   25 E5
Bampton Cl MK4   29 E3
Banburies Cl MK18   29 G2
Bank Ho MK9   4 C5
Banktop Pl MK4   28 C2
Bantock Cl MK7   25 G6
Barbers Mews MK14   17 F3
Barbury Ct MK14   13 G6
Bardsey Ct MK10   25 E1
Barford MK11   20 C1
Barkers Cft MK12   21 E1
Barkestone Cl MK4   28 C4

Barleycorn Cl LU7   39 H2
Barleycroft MK4   29 E1
Barnabas Rd LU7   38 B3
Barnfield Dr MK6   23 H6
Barnsbury Gdns MK16   14 A3
Barnsdale Dr MK4   27 F5
Barons Cl MK2   29 H5
Barrett Pl MK5   26 F1
Barrington Mews MK6   5 F6
Barry Av MK13   16 B3
Bartholomew Cl MK7   24 D6
Bartlett Pl MK18   3 D3
Barton Rd MK2   34 A1
Bascote MK6   24 B6
Basildon Ct,
  Leighton Buzzard LU7   38 D2
Basildon Ct,
  Milton Keynes MK8   21 H5
Baskerfield Gro MK6   24 A3
Bassett Ct,
  Leighton Buzzard LU7   39 E2
Bassett Ct,
  Newport Pagnell MK16   14 A3
Bassett Rd LU7   38 D3
Bateman Cft MK5   26 F1
Bates Cl MK15   18 B1
Bath La MK18   3 A5
Bath Lane Ter MK18   3 A4
Baxter Cl MK8   21 H5
Bay Tree Cl MK17   32 D3
Bayard Av MK14   17 F4
Baynham Mead MK7   25 E2
Beacon Ct MK4   28 D3
Beaconsfield Pl MK16   14 A3
Beadlemead MK6   23 H4
Beales La MK7   24 D6
Beanfare MK6   23 H4
Beauchamp Cl MK14   17 E2
Beaudesert LU7   39 E2
Beaufort Dr MK15   18 A1
Beaumaris Gro MK5   22 B4
Beaver Cl MK18   3 C5
Beaverbrook Ct MK3   29 F4
Bec La MK15   17 H1
Beckinsale Gro MK8   21 G6
Beddoes Cft MK5   26 E3
Bedford Rd MK17   36 E2
Bedford St,
  Fenny Stratford MK2   30 A5
Bedford St,
  Leighton Buzzard LU7   39 E2
Bedford St,
  Wolverton MK12   11 F5
Bedgebury Pl MK7   25 E2
Beech Cl MK18   3 B2
Beech Gro LU7   38 C2
Beech House Dr NN12   8 B1
Beech Tree Cl MK19   11 G1
Beechcroft Rd MK3   33 E1
Beethoven Cl MK7   25 H6
Beeward Cl MK12   10 D6
Bekonscot Ct MK14   13 F5
Bell Alley LU7   39 E3
Bellfounder Ho MK13   16 B5
Bellini Cl MK7   25 G6
Bellis Gro MK6   24 A3
Bells Mdw MK15   17 H2
Bellwether MK11   20 C2
Belmont Ct MK8   21 F4
Belsize Av MK6   23 H1
Belvedere La MK17   30 C4
Belvoir Av MK4   28 C4
Benacre Cft MK4   28 C4
Benbow Ct MK5   22 A4
Bennet Cl MK11   20 A1
Bens Cl MK19   6 B2
Benstall Cl MK15   18 A1
Benwell Cl MK13   16 A4
Berberis Cl MK7   25 E5
Bercham MK8   21 H3
Beresford Cl MK4   28 C1
Beretun MK8   21 G4
Bereville Ct MK10   18 C6
Berevilles La MK10   18 B6
Bergamot Gdns MK7   25 F5
Berkshire Grn MK5   26 F4
Berling Rd MK8   21 H3
Bernardines Way MK18   3 C5
Bernay Gdns MK15   17 G1
Bernstein Cl MK7   31 G1
Berry La MK17   36 E1
Berry Way MK17   32 D3
Berrystead MK7   31 E2
Bertram Cl MK18   3 A3
Berwald Cl MK7   31 G1
Berwick Dr MK3   29 F3
Bessemer Ct MK14   13 G5
Bettina Gro MK2   30 A6
Betty's Cl MK17   32 D3
Beverley Pl MK6   23 H1
Bewdley Dr LU7   38 A3

Bickleigh Cres MK4   28 C2
Bideford Ct LU7   38 B2
Bideford Grn LU7   38 A1
Bignell Cft MK5   22 B2
Bilbrook La MK4   28 C1
Billington Ct LU7   39 E4
Billington Rd LU7   39 F4
Billingwell Pl MK6   17 H6
Bilton Rd MK1   30 B3
Bingham Cl MK4   28 C4
Birch Ho MK14   16 C3
Birchen Lee MK4   28 C3
Birchfield Gro MK2   30 A5
Birdlip La MK7   25 E4
Bird's Hill LU7   37 C2
Birkdale Cl MK3   28 D6
Bishop Cl LU7   39 H4
Bishops Cl MK18   3 A5
Bishops Walk MK17   36 B3
Bishopstone MK13   16 B3
Blackberry Ct MK7   25 F5
Blackdown MK11   20 C1
Blackham Cl MK6   23 E3
Blackheath Cres MK13   4 C1
Blackhill Dr MK12   10 C5
Blackmoor Gate MK4   28 D3
Blackthorn Gro MK17   36 A2
Blackwell Pl MK5   28 A1
Blackwood Cres MK13   11 H5
Blairmont St MK9   17 F5
Blakedown Rd LU7   38 A3
Blakeney Cl MK4   28 B5
Blanchland Circle MK10   24 D1
Blansby Chase MK4   28 C2
Blatherwick Ct MK5   21 H6
Blaydon Cl MK3   32 D1
Bleasdale MK13   16 C3
Blenheim Av MK11   20 B1
Bletcham Way MK1   29 H2
Bletchley Rd,
  Newton Longville
  MK17   32 D5
Bletchley Rd,
  Shenley Brook End
  MK5   28 B1
Blind Pond
  Ind Est MK17   31 G3
Bliss Ct MK7   25 F6
Blisworth MK6   24 A5
Bluebell Cl MK18   3 A5
Bluebell Ct MK7   25 F4
Blundells Rd MK13   16 B3
Blyth Cl MK4   28 A4
Blythe Cl MK14   14 B3
Bodenham Cl MK18   3 D4
Bodiam Cl MK5   22 A6
Bodle Cl MK15   17 G2
Bolan Ct MK8   26 E1
Bolton Cl MK3   29 G3
Boltwood Gro MK5   26 F2
Bond Av MK1   30 B1
Bonnards Rd MK17   32 D3
Booker Av MK13   4 B1
Borodin Cl MK7   25 G6
Borough Walk MK9   5 E2
Bossard Ct LU7   39 E3
Bossiney Pl MK6   5 G4
Bossington La LU7   38 D3
Bostock Cft MK18   3 A3
Boswell Ct MK18   3 C2
Bosworth Cl MK3   29 E3
Bottesford Cl MK4   28 D4
Boulters Lock MK14   13 F5
Boundary Cres MK11   10 B6
Bounds Cft MK12   21 E1
Bourton Rd MK16   3 B4
Bourtonville MK18   3 C5
Bouverie Sq MK9   4 C4
Bow Brickhill Rd MK17   36 A3
Bowback Ho MK9   4 C4
Bowen Cl MK7   25 G6
Bowes Cl MK16   14 A3
Bowland Dr MK4   28 B4
Bowles Pl MK6   24 B3
Bowling Leys MK10   18 D6
Bowood Ct MK8   21 H5
Bowyers Mews MK14   17 F3
Boxberry Gdns MK7   25 E5
Boxgrove Ct MK10   24 D1
Boyce Cres MK7   25 G6
Boycott Av MK6   5 E6
Brackley Rd MK18   3 A3
Bradbourne Dr MK7   31 E2
Bradbury Cl MK13   16 A5
Bradfield Av MK18   3 B2
Bradley Gro MK4   28 C3
Bradvue Cres MK13   16 B2
Bradwell Common Blvd
  MK13   4 A2

Bradwell Rd,
  Bradwell MK13   16 A1
Bradwell Rd,
  Loughton Lodge MK5,8   22 A1
Braford Gdns MK5   22 B6
Bragenham La LU7   37 A3
Bragenham Side MK17   7 C5
Brahms Cl MK7   25 G5
Bramber Cl MK3   29 E6
Bramble Av MK14   17 E4
Bramble Cl LU7   39 G3
Bramley Mdws MK16   13 G3
Bramley Rd MK1   30 A2
Brampton Ct MK13   16 A3
Bransgill Ct MK13   16 B4
Bransworth Av MK7   25 G3
Brantham Cl MK7   31 E2
Braunston MK6   24 B5
Braybrooke Dr MK4   29 E1
Brayton Ct MK5   22 C5
Breamore Cl MK8   21 G6
Brearley Av MK6   23 E4
Breckland MK14   16 C3
Brecon Cl MK10   24 D1
Bremen Gro MK5   28 A1
Brendon Ct MK4   29 E2
Brent MK6   24 B6
Bretby Chase MK4   26 F4
Breton MK11   10 B5
Briar Hill MK12   11 G6
Briar Lodge MK12   21 G1
Briary Vw MK17   27 C7
Brices Mdw MK5   28 A2
Brick Cl MK11   21 E3
Brickhill Manor Ct MK17   35 G2
Brickhill St,
  Bow Brickhill MK7   31 E3
Brickhill St,
  Great Linford MK14,15   13 F4
Brickhill St,
  Monkston MK10,17   24 C1
Bridge Rd MK19   10 B1
Bridge St,
  Buckingham MK18   3 B4
Bridge St,
  Leighton Buzzard LU7   38 D3
Bridge St,
  New Bradwell MK13   16 A1
Bridgeford Ct MK6   23 E2
Bridgeturn Av MK12   11 F4
Bridgnorth Dr MK5   16 A1
Bridle Cl MK13   16 B3
Bridlington Cres MK10   24 D2
Brill Pl MK13   4 A2
Brindlebrook MK8   21 G4
Brinkburn Chase MK10   24 D1
Bristle Hill MK18   3 B4
Bristow Cl MK2   30 B4
Britten Gro MK7   25 G5
Broad Arrow Ct MK14   17 E2
Broad Dean MK6   23 G3
Broad St MK16   13 H3
Broadlands MK6   23 H5
Broadpiece MK15   17 G2
Broadwater MK6   24 B5
Broadway Av MK14   13 F4
Brockwell MK16   14 A3
Bromham Mill MK14   13 F5
Brook Cl MK17   7 C5
Brook St LU7   39 G2
Brook Way MK19   9 A8
Brooke Cl MK3   29 F6
Brookfield La MK18   3 B5
Brookfield Rd,
  Haversham MK19   11 F1
Brookfield Rd,
  Newton Longville
  MK17   32 D4
Brooklands Av LU7   39 F3
Brooklands Dr LU7   39 F3
Brooklands Rd MK2   30 A5
Brooks Ct MK18   3 B4
Brookside Cl MK19   9 E6
Brookside Walk LU7   39 G2
Broomfield MK12   21 G1
Broomlee MK13   16 A3
Broomshill Rd LU7   39 E1
Brora Cl MK7   34 A2
Brough Cl MK5   22 A6
Broughton Manor
  Bsns Pk MK16   19 E5
Broughton Rd,
  Broughton MK10   19 E6
Broughton Rd,
  Milton Keynes Village
  MK10   18 D6
Brownbaker Ct MK14   17 F3
Browne Willis Cl MK2   30 B5
Browning Cl MK16   13 G2
Browning Cres MK3   29 F6

40

Haddington Cl MK3 29 E2
Haddon MK8 21 H5
Hadley Pl MK13 4 B2
Hadrians Dr MK13 16 A3
Hainault Av MK14 13 G5
Haithwaite MK8 21 G4
Haldene MK8 21 G3
Hale Av MK11 20 B1
Hall Cl, Buckingham MK18 3 D1
Hall Cl, Old Stratford MK19 9 E6
Halswell Pl MK10 19 E6
Haltonchesters MK13 16 A3
Haly Cl MK13 16 B5
Hambleton Gro MK4 28 B3
Hamburg Cft MK5 28 B2
Hamilton Ct LU7 39 E2
Hamilton La MK3 32 C1
Hamlins MK6 23 F5
Hammerwood Gate MK7 24 D4
Hammond Cres MK15 17 H2
Hampson Cl MK13 16 B4
Hampstead Gate MK13 4 B2
Hampton MK8 22 A2
Handel Mead MK7 25 H6
Hanmer Rd MK6 24 B6
Hanover Ct, Leighton Buzzard LU7 38 B3
Hanover Ct, Stantonbury MK14 16 D1
Hanscomb Cl MK15 18 A6
Hanslope Rd, Castlethorpe MK19 6 B1
Hanslope Rd, Hanslope MK19 7 B3
Harborne Ct MK8 21 F4
Harby Cl MK4 28 C4
Harcourt MK13 16 A6
Harcourt Cl LU7 38 D2
Harding Rd MK7 25 G3
Hardwick Mews MK17 36 B3
Hardwick Pl MK17 36 B3
Hardwick Rd MK17 36 B3
Hare Cl MK18 3 C5
Harebell Cl MK7 25 E6
Hareden Cft MK4 28 B3
Hargreaves Nook MK14 13 G5
Harkness Cl MK2 34 A1
Harland Ho MK9 4 B4
Harlans Cl MK6 23 H3
Harlech Pl MK3 29 E6
Harlequin Pl MK5 26 F4
Harlestone Ct MK14 13 G6
Harmill Ind Est LU7 39 E5
Harmony Row LU7 39 H4
Harnett Dr MK12 10 C5
Harpers La MK14 17 F1
Harrier Ct MK6 23 G2
Harrier Dr MK6 23 G3
Harrison Cl MK5 22 D5
Harrow Rd LU7 39 F4
Harrowden MK13 16 B1
Hartdames MK5 28 B2
Hartfield Cl MK7 25 E3
Hartington Gro MK4 28 B2
Hartland Av MK4 28 B5
Hartley MK14 13 E6
Hartwell Cres LU7 39 F3
Hartwell Gro LU7 39 E3
Hartwort Cl MK7 25 E5
Harvard Cl MK14 13 E4
Harvester Cl MK12 10 D6
Harvester Ct LU7 39 H3
Harwood St MK13 16 A1
Hasgill Ct MK13 16 C4
Haslow Ct MK8 21 G3
Hastings MK11 10 B6
Hatchlands MK8 21 H4
Hathaway Ct MK8 21 G6
Hatton MK6 24 B5
Hauksbee Gdns MK5 22 D6
Haversham Rd MK19 11 F2
Hawker Cl LU7 39 H4
Hawkhurst Gate MK7 24 D3
Hawkins Cl MK11 10 A6
Hawkmoor Cl MK6 23 H3
Hawkridge MK4 29 E2
Hawkshead Dr MK4 28 C2
Hawkwell Est MK19 9 E5
Hawthorn Av MK2 30 C5
Hawthorne Cl LU7 38 C2
Haydock Cl MK3 32 C1
Hayes Rd MK19 9 B7
Hayman Rise MK8 26 D1
Haynes Cl MK17 31 G3
Haythrop Cl MK15 17 G2
Haywards Cft MK12 11 E6
Hazel Gro MK2 30 A6
Hazel Row MK19 7 C2
Hazelwood MK14 17 F1
Hazley Walk MK18 3 D3
Heaney Cl MK16 13 G1
Hearne Pl MK6 23 F3
Heath Cl MK17 36 C3
Heath Ct LU7 37 A4
Heath Grn LU7 37 C3
Heath Park Dr LU7 37 C5
Heath Park Rd LU7 37 C5
Heath Rd, Great Brickhill MK17 35 G6
Heath Rd, Leighton Buzzard LU7 39 E1
Heathcroft Ho MK14 17 E2
Heathercroft MK14 17 E1
Heathfield MK12 21 G1
Heathwood Cl LU7 37 C5
Hedges Ct MK5 22 B5
Hedingham Ct MK5 22 A6
Hele Ct MK7 31 E2
Helford Pl MK6 23 G1
Helmsley Rise MK4 27 E6
Helston Pl MK6 5 H6
Hemingway Cl MK16 13 F2
Henders MK11 20 B1
Hendrix Dr MK8 21 G6
Hengistbury La MK4 28 A4
Hensman Gate MK15 18 C5
Hepleswell MK8 21 G5
Hercules Cl LU7 39 G2
Herdman Cl MK12 11 E6
Heron Ho MK7 24 D3
Herriot Cl MK16 13 G2
Hertford Pl MK3 29 F3
Hesketh Rd NN12 6 B5
Hexham Gdns MK3 32 D1
Heybridge Cres MK7 31 E2
Heydon Ct MK13 16 A1
Higgs Ct MK5 22 A2
High Halden MK7 25 E3
High Park Dr MK12 10 D5
High St, Buckingham MK18 3 B3
High St, Deanshanger MK19 9 B8
High St, Great Linford MK14 13 E6
High St, Hanslope MK19 7 C2
High St, Leighton Buzzard LU7 39 E3
High St, New Bradwell MK13 16 A1
High St, Newport Pagnell MK16 14 A2
High St, Potterspury NN12 8 A1
High St, Stony Stratford MK11 9 F6
High St, Whaddon MK17 27 B6
High St, Woburn Sands MK17 36 B3
High St, Yardley Gobin NN12 6 C5
High Street Mews LU7 39 E3
High Trees MK6 23 H2
High Vw MK19 9 A7
Higham Cross Rd MK19 7 A1
Highbury La MK9 17 G6
Highclere Ho MK14 17 F3
Highcroft LU7 39 G4
Highcroft Cl NN12 6 B5
Highfield Cl, Milton Keynes MK3 29 G3
Highfield Cl, Newport Pagnell MK16 14 C3
Highfield Rd LU7 39 G3
Highgate Over MK7 25 E4
Highgrove Hill MK8 21 H5
Highland Cl MK3 29 F2
Highlands Rd MK18 3 C2
Highley Gro MK10 19 E6
Highveer Cft MK4 28 B4
Hill Vw MK16 13 G3
Hillbeck Gro MK10 18 C5
Hillcrest Cl MK5 22 C4
Hillcrest Rise MK18 3 C6
Hillesden Way MK18 3 C3
Hilliard Dr MK13 16 A6
Hills Cl MK14 17 E2
Hillside Rd LU7 37 C6
Hilltop Av MK18 3 C2
Hillway MK17 36 A1
Himley Grn LU7 38 B3
Hindemith Gdns MK7 25 G6
Hindhead Knoll MK7 25 F5
Hinton Cl LU7 39 G3
Hinton Ct MK3 29 F4
Hoathly Mews MK7 25 E2
Hobart Cres MK15 17 H2
Hockliffe Brae MK7 25 F6
Hockliffe Rd LU7 39 F3
Hockliffe St LU7 39 E3
Hodder La MK4 28 C2
Hodge Lea La MK12 21 F1
Hodgemore Ct MK14 13 F4
Hogarths Ct MK8 21 H4
Holborn Cres MK4 28 A5
Holdom Av MK1 30 B3
Holland Way MK16 13 H4
Holliday Cl MK8 26 E1
Hollies Ct LU7 38 D3
Hollin La MK12 21 G1
Hollinwell Cl MK3 28 D4
Hollister Chase MK5 28 B1
Holloway Dr MK18 3 C2
Holly Cl MK8 26 F1
Holly Walk MK17 36 B4
Holm Gate MK5 22 A2
Holmewood MK4 29 E1
Holmfield Cl MK6 24 B5
Holst Cres MK7 25 G6
Holt Gro MK5 22 A2
Holton Hill MK4 28 C3
Holton Rd MK18 3 B2
Holts Grn MK17 35 G6
Holy Thorn La MK5 22 A5
Holyhead Cres MK4 28 C5
Holyrood MK8 21 H5
Holywell Pl MK6 17 H6
Home Cl, Milton Keynes MK3 29 G3
Home Cl, Towcester NN12 6 C5
Home Farm La MK17 35 G5
Home Fld MK7 31 E1
Homeground MK18 3 C6
Homeridings Ho MK13 16 B4
Homestall MK18 3 C6
Homestall Cl MK5 22 A3
Homestead Way NN12 8 A1
Homeward Ct MK5 22 B4
Honey Hill Dr MK19 9 B7
Honeypot Cl MK13 16 B5
Hooper Gate MK15 18 A1
Hopkins Cl MK10 18 D6
Hoppers Mdw MK5 22 A3
Hopton Gro MK16 14 C4
Horn La MK11 10 A6
Hornbeam MK16 13 G4
Hornbeam Cl LU7 39 G1
Hornbeam Ct MK6 24 A4
Hornby Chase MK4 28 B3
Horners Cft MK12 11 F6
Horsefair Grn MK11 10 A6
Horton Gate MK14 13 F5
Hortonsfield Rd NN12 6 C6
Horwood Ct MK1 30 B3
Houghton Ct MK8 21 H5
Housman Cl MK16 13 G1
Howard Way MK16 14 D3
Howe Ct MK10 18 D6
Howe Park Ho MK4 28 A4
Howe Rock Pl MK4 28 B4
Hoylake Cl MK3 28 D6
Hoyton Gate MK8 26 E1
Hubbard Cl MK18 3 D3
Huckleberry Cl MK7 25 F5
Hudson La MK8 21 G6
Hugh Park Cl MK5 22 C3
Humber Way MK3 29 E4
Hungerford Ho MK4 28 D3
Hunsdon Cl MK14 16 D2
Hunstanton Way MK3 28 D5
Hunter Dr MK2 30 A6
Hunter St MK18 3 A5
Hunters Reach MK13 16 A5
Huntingbrooke MK8 21 H5
Huntingdon Cres MK3 28 C6
Huntley Cres MK9 17 G5
Huntsman Gro MK14 13 G5
Hurley Cft MK10 25 E1
Hurlstone Gro MK4 28 D2
Hutchings Cl MK5 22 A3
Hutton Av MK6 5 F6
Hutton Ct MK17 36 B2
Hutton Way MK17 36 B1
Huxley Cl MK16 13 F2
Hyde Cl MK16 14 A4
Hydrus Dr LU7 39 H1

Ibstone Av MK13 16 C5
Illingworth Pl MK6 23 E3
Innes Ct MK8 26 E1
Innholder Ct MK14 17 F3
Inverness Cl MK3 29 F3
Ireland Cl MK7 31 G1
Ironmonger Ct MK14 17 F3
Irving Dale MK7 25 H6
Isaacson Dr MK7 25 F4
Isis Walk LU7 37 D4
Islingbrook MK5 28 B1
Iver Ct MK18 3 A5
Ivester Ct LU7 38 C3
Ivy Cl MK16 14 C3
Ivy La, Great Brickhill MK17 35 F6
Ivy La, Newton Longville MK17 32 C4

Jacobs Cl MK14 16 D2
Japonica La MK15 18 A3
Jarman Cl MK18 3 D4
Jeeves Cl MK6 23 H3
Jenkins Cl MK5 26 F2
Jenna Way MK16 14 D3
Jennings MK14 16 C1
Jerrard Cl LU7 39 G4
Jersey Rd MK12 11 E4
Johnson Dr LU7 39 F5
Johnston Pl MK6 5 E6
Jonathans MK6 23 G5
Jonathans Ct MK6 23 G5
Joplin Ct MK8 26 F1
Joules Ct MK5 22 C6
Jubilee Ter MK11 10 A6
Judges La LU7 38 D3
Juniper Gdns MK7 25 F4
Jupiter Dr LU7 39 H2

Kalman Gdns MK7 25 G6
Kaplan Cl MK5 22 C6
Katherine Cl MK7 30 D1
Katrine Pl MK2 34 B2
Keaton Cl MK8 26 E1
Keats Cl MK16 13 G3
Keats Way MK3 29 F6
Kellan Dr MK6 23 G1
Keller Cl MK11 21 E3
Kelsey Cl MK4 28 A5
Kelso Cl MK3 32 D1
Kelvin Dr MK5 22 D5
Kemble Ct MK15 17 G3
Kempton Gdns MK3 32 D1
Kenchester MK13 21 H1
Kendal Gdns LU7 38 B3
Kendall Pl MK5 26 F2
Kenilworth Dr MK3 29 E5
Kennedy Ct LU7 39 E2
Kennet Dr MK3 29 E5
Kennington Cl MK16 13 H4
Kensington Dr MK8 21 H4
Kents Rd MK14 16 D1
Kenwell Ct MK15 18 A6
Kenwood Gate MK6 17 H6
Keppel Av MK19 11 G1
Kepwick MK8 21 H4
Kercroft MK8 21 G3
Kernow Cres MK6 5 H5
Kerria Pl MK3 29 G2
Kersey MK14 16 C1
Kestrel Ho MK7 24 D2
Kestrel Way MK18 3 D5
Keswick Rd MK19 7 C2
Ketelbey Nook MK7 25 H6
Ketton Cl MK15 18 B1
Kew Ct MK8 21 H4
Keyes Way MK18 3 C2
Keynes Cl MK16 14 C2
Khasiaberry MK7 25 E6
Kidd Cl MK8 26 E1
Kidderminster Walk MK10 19 E6
Kildonan Pl MK12 21 F1
Kilkenny Ho MK4 27 E5
Kiln Farm Ind Est MK11 20 D2
Kilwinning Dr MK10 24 D2
Kimbolton Ct MK14 17 G1
Kincardine Dr MK3 29 E2
Kindermann Ct MK5 22 B6
Kindleton MK14 17 F1
King Charles Cl MK18 3 C2
King Edward St MK13 11 H4
King George Cres MK11 10 A5
King St, Leighton Buzzard LU7 39 E1
King St, Stony Stratford MK11 10 A5
Kingfisher Ho MK7 24 D3
Kingfisher Rd MK18 3 D5
Kingsbridge MK4 28 D2
Kingsfold MK13 16 B2
Kingshill Dr MK19 9 B7
Kingsley Cl MK16 13 F2
Kingsoe Leys MK10 19 E6
Kingston Av MK11 10 B6
Kinloch Pl MK2 34 B2
Kinnear Cl MK8 21 G6
Kinross Dr MK3 29 E3
Kipling Dr MK16 13 F3
Kipling Rd MK3 29 G6
Kirke Cl MK5 22 A5
Kirkeby Cl MK14 16 D2
Kirkham Ct MK5 22 C3
Kirkstall Pl MK6 4 D6
Kirkwood Gro MK5 26 D2
Kirtlington MK15 17 G3
Kitelee Cl MK19 7 B1
Kiteleys Grn LU7 39 G2
Knapp Gate MK5 21 H6
Knaresborough Ct MK3 28 D6
Knaves Hill LU7 38 B2
Knights Cl MK17 35 G6
Knowl Gate MK5 22 C3
Knowles Grn MK2 30 A5
Knox Bri MK7 25 E2
Kramer Ct MK8 26 E1
Krohn Cl MK18 3 D4
Krypton Cl MK5 22 C5

Laburnum Ct LU7 39 E2
Laburnum Gro MK2 30 B5
Lacy Dr MK15 17 G1
Ladymead Cl MK17 27 B7
Ladymeadow Ct MK10 18 C6
Laggan Ct MK2 34 B3
Lagonda Cl MK16 14 C2
Laidon Cl MK2 34 B2
Lake St LU7 39 E3
Laker Ct MK6 23 E4
Lakes La MK16 13 F1
Lamb Cl MK16 13 F2
Lamb La MK7 25 F4
Lamberhurst Gro MK7 25 E2
Lamberts Cft MK12 21 F1
Lambourn Ct MK4 28 D3
Lammas MK6 23 G6
Lammas Walk LU7 39 E2
Lampitts Cross MK6 23 H5
Lamport Ct MK8 22 A2
Lamsey Ct LU7 39 E2
Lancaster Gate MK3 29 E6
Landrace Ct MK5 28 A2
Lands End Gro MK4 27 F7
Landsborough Gate MK15 18 A2
Lanercost Cres MK10 25 E1
Lane's End LU7 37 C3
Lanfranc Gdns MK15 17 H1
Langcliffe Dr MK13 16 B4
Langdale Cl MK2 34 A3
Langerstone La MK4 28 B4
Langford Pl MK7 31 E2
Langland Rd MK6 24 A4
Langmuir Ct MK5 28 C1
Langney Grn MK4 28 A4
Langton Dr MK8 21 G3
Lanthorn Cl MK14 17 E2
Lapwing Ho MK7 24 D3
Larch Gro MK2 30 B6
Larch Ho MK14 16 C3
Lark Cl MK18 3 D5
Larkin Cl MK16 13 G1
Larkspur Av MK14 17 E4
Larwood Pl MK6 5 G6
Lasborough Rd MK10 25 F2
Lascelles Cl MK15 17 H1
Laser Cl MK5 22 C5
Lastingham Gro MK4 28 B2
Lathwell Way LU7 39 F5
Latimer MK11 20 B1
Launceston Ct MK5 22 B5
Launde MK10 25 E1
Laura Dro MK14 13 G4
Laurel Cl MK8 26 E1
Lavender Gro MK7 25 E6
Lawnsmead Gdns MK16 14 A2
Lawson Pl MK5 22 B6
Leafield Rise MK8 21 G4
Learoyd Way LU7 39 H4
Leary Cres MK16 14 C3
Leasowe Pl MK13 4 A2
Ledburn Gro LU7 38 C4
Ledbury MK14 13 E6
Leedon Furlong LU7 39 G3
Leigh Hill MK4 28 D3
Leighton Rd, Heath and Reach LU7 37 C4
Leighton Rd, Leedon LU7 39 H2
Leighton Rd, Leighton Buzzard LU7 38 D3
Leighton Rd, Linslade LU7 38 A1
Leighton Rd, Stoke Hammond MK17 7 C5
Lenborough Cl MK18 3 B5
Lenborough Ct MK15 24 A1
Lenborough Rd MK18 3 A5
Lennon Dr MK8 26 E1
Lennox Rd MK2 30 A5
Lenthall Cl MK13 16 A4
Leominster Gate MK10 24 D2
Leon Av MK2 30 A5
Leonards Lee MK4 27 F5
Leopard Dr MK15 17 G2
Leopold Rd LU7 38 C2
Leven Cl, Leighton Buzzard LU7 38 A3
Leven Cl, Water Eaton MK2 34 B2
Lewes Ho MK3 28 D6
Lewis Cl MK16 13 F2
Leyland Pl MK6 5 F6
Leys Rd MK5 22 B3
Lichfield Down MK7 25 E6
Liddell Way LU7 39 H4
Lightfoot Ct MK7 24 D6
Lilac Cl MK17 32 C4
Lilleshall Av MK10 24 D2
Limbaud Cl MK7 24 D6
Lime Av MK18 3 D5
Lime Cl MK16 13 H3
Lime Gro, Leighton Buzzard LU7 38 D2
Lime Gro, Milton Keynes MK17 36 B3
Lime Rd NN12 6 B5
Limerick La MK9 17 H6
Linceslade Gro MK5 22 A3
Lincoln MK14 16 C1
Lincoln Ct MK19 7 C2
Lincombe Slade LU7 38 C2
Linden Gro MK14 13 E6
Lindisfarne Dr MK10 25 E1
Lindler Ct LU7 39 E4
Lindores Cft MK10 25 E2
Linford Av MK16 13 G3
Linford Ct MK19 12 C2
Linford La, Willen MK15 18 A1
Linford La, Woolstone MK15 18 A5

Lingfield MK12 21 G1
Linney Ct MK4 28 A4
Linslade Rd LU7 37 A3
Lintlaw Pl MK3 29 G2
Linwood Gro LU7 39 F4
Lipscomb La MK5 22 A4
Lipscombe Dr MK18 3 C3
Lissel Rd MK6 24 B6
Little Balmer MK18 3 C6
Little Dunmow MK10 25 E1
Little Habton MK4 28 B2
Little Hame MK10 18 D5
Little Linford La,
 Milton Keynes MK19 12 C1
Little Linford La,
 Newport Pagnell MK16 13 F3
Little London MK19 9 A7
Little Mdw MK5 22 B4
Little Stanton MK14 16 D1
Little Stocking MK5 28 A1
Littlecote MK8 22 A2
Littlemere MK8 21 G4
Livesey Hill MK5 22 B5
Livingstone Dr MK15 18 A4
Lloyds MK6 23 F4
Lloyd's Ct MK9 5 E1
Lochy Dr LU7 38 A2
Lock La MK19 10 B1
Lock View La MK1 30 C4
Locke Rd MK2 29 H5
Lockton Ct MK4 28 C2
Lodge Farm Ct MK19 6 B1
Lodge Gate MK14 17 E1
Lodge La MK17 7 B5
Logan Rock MK4 28 B4
Lomond Dr,
 Leighton Buzzard LU7 38 A3
Lomond Dr,
 Milton Keynes MK2 34 A4
London End MK17 32 D3
London End La MK17 31 G4
London Rd,
 Broughton MK10 19 E4
London Rd,
 Buckingham MK18 3 B4
London Rd,
 Loughton MK5 22 A4
London Rd,
 Newport Pagnell MK16 14 C3
London Rd,
 Old Stratford MK19 9 E5
London Rd,
 Stony Stratford MK11 10 A6
Long Ayres MK7 31 E2
Long Street Rd MK19 7 B1
Longcross MK15 17 G2
Longfellow Dr MK16 13 G2
Longhedge MK7 31 E2
Longleat Ct MK8 21 H4
Longpeak Cl MK4 28 B4
Longville MK12 10 D4
Lords Cl MK2 30 A4
Loriner Pl MK14 17 G3
Loseley Ct MK8 21 H4
Lothersdale MK13 16 B3
Lothian Cl MK3 29 E3
Lotsgill Ct MK13 16 C4
Loughton Rd MK13 16 A5
Lovat St MK16 14 A3
Lovatt Dr MK3 29 E5
Lovent Dr LU7 39 F3
Lower Eighth St MK9 5 F3
Lower End MK17 32 C4
Lower Fourth St MK9 4 C5
Lower Ninth St MK9 5 F3
Lower Second St MK9 4 C5
Lower Stonehayes MK14 17 F1
Lower Tenth St MK9 5 F2
Lower Third St MK9 4 C5
Lower Twelfth St MK9 5 G2
Lower Way MK17 35 F5
Lower Wharf MK18 3 C3
Lowick Pl MK4 28 C4
Lowland Rd MK4 28 C4
Lowndes Gro MK5 21 H6
Loxbeare Dr MK4 28 C1
Lucas Pl MK6 24 B3
Lucy La MK5 22 B2
Ludlow Cl MK3 29 F6
Lufford Pk MK14 13 F6
Luke Pl MK10 18 C5
Lullingstone Dr MK13 11 H6
Lundholme MK13 16 B4
Luttlemarsh MK7 24 D6
Lutyens Gro MK7 25 G6
Lydiard MK8 21 H5
Lynmouth Cres MK4 28 C1
Lynott Cl MK8 26 E1
Lyon Rd MK1 29 H3
Lyra Gdns LU7 39 H2
Lywood Rd LU7 39 G4

Maclaren Ct MK6 23 F3
Mag St MK9 22 D1
Magdalen Cl MK11 10 A5
Magdalen Ho MK11 10 A5
Magenta Cl MK4 34 A1
Magpie Cl MK5 28 B1

Mahler Cl MK7 25 F6
Maidenhead Av MK13 4 A1
Maidstone Rd MK10 25 F1
Main St, Cosgrove MK19 10 B1
Main St,
 Maids Moreton MK18 3 D1
Malborough Way NN12 6 C6
Malins Gate MK14 17 E1
Mallard Dr MK18 3 C4
Malletts Cl MK11 10 B6
Mallow Gate MK14 17 E5
Maltings Fld MK19 6 C2
Malton Cl MK10 24 D2
Malvern Dr,
 Leighton Buzzard LU7 38 A1
Malvern Dr,
 Milton Keynes MK11 20 C1
Mandeville Dr MK10 25 F1
Manifold La MK4 28 B2
Mannock Way LU7 39 H4
Manor Cl,
 Aspley Guise MK17 36 E2
Manor Cl,
 Cosgrove MK19 10 A1
Manor Cl, Hanslope MK19 7 C2
Manor Cl,
 Milton Keynes Village
 MK10 18 D6
Manor Cl,
 Stoke Hammond MK17 7 C5
Manor Dr MK19 11 G1
Manor Gdns MK18 3 C2
Manor Rd,
 Fenny Stratford MK2 30 B6
Manor Rd,
 Newport Pagnell MK16 13 G3
Manor Rd,
 Newton Longville
 MK17 32 D4
Manor Rd,
 Wolverton MK12 10 D4
Manor St MK18 3 B4
Manorfields Rd MK19 9 E6
Manse Cl MK11 10 A5
Mansel Cl MK10 10 A1
Mansell Cl MK5 22 A4
Manshead Ct MK11 10 B6
Mapeley Ho MK15 18 C5
Maple Gro,
 Fenny Stratford MK2 30 B6
Maple Gro,
 Woburn Sands MK17 36 A2
Mapledean MK12 21 G1
Mapledurham MK7 31 E2
Mara Pl MK9 17 G5
March Mdw MK7 25 G6
Marconi Cft MK5 22 C6
Mardle Rd LU7 38 D4
Mare Leys MK18 3 D4
Maree Cl,
 Leighton Buzzard LU7 38 A2
Maree Cl,
 Milton Keynes MK2 34 A2
Margam Cres MK10 25 E2
Margaret Powell Sq MK9 5 G1
Marigold Pl MK14 17 E4
Marina Dr MK12 11 F6
Marjoram Pl MK14 17 E4
Markenfield Pl MK4 27 E6
Market Hill MK18 3 B3
Market Mews LU7 39 E3
Market Sq,
 Buckingham MK18 3 B4
Market Sq,
 Hanslope MK19 7 C2
Market Sq,
 Stony Stratford MK11 10 A6
Markhams Cl MK18 3 B4
Marlborough Gate MK9 5 H2
Marlborough St,
 Milton Keynes MK6 23 H2
Marlborough St,
 Stantonbury MK14 16 C1
Marley Flds LU7 39 G3
Marley Gro MK8 26 E1
Marlow Dr MK16 13 G2
Marlowe MK3 23 G6
Marron La MK12 11 F6
Marsh Dr MK14 13 E4
Marsh End Rd MK16 14 A3
Marshall Ct
 Ind Pk MK1 29 H4
Marshalls La MK15 18 A6
Marshaw Pl MK4 28 C3
Marshworth MK6 24 B5
Martell Cl MK7 31 E1
Martella Ho MK13 16 B6
Martin Cl,
 Buckingham MK18 3 D5
Martin Cl,
 Milton Keynes MK14 17 E2
Martingale Pl MK14 17 F4
Marwood Cl MK4 28 D2
Mary MacManus Dr
 MK18 3 B3
Maryland Rd MK15 13 H6
Masefield Cl MK16 13 G3
Masefield Gro MK3 29 F4

Maslin Dr MK6 23 G5
Mason MK14 16 C1
Massie Cl MK15 17 H2
Mathiesen Rd MK13 16 A3
Matilda Gdns MK5 22 B5
Matthew Cr MK5 22 B5
Maudslay Cl MK5 22 C5
Mauduit Rd MK19 7 C1
Maulden Gdns MK14 13 G6
Mavoncliff Dr MK4 28 B5
Maxham MK5 28 B2
Maybach Cl MK5 22 B6
Mayditch Pl MK13 16 C5
Mayer Gdns MK5 22 C6
Maynard Cl MK13 16 B6
Mays Way NN12 8 A1
McConnell Dr MK12 11 G4
McKenzie Cl MK18 3 B4
Meadow Cres MK5 22 B4
Meadow Gdns MK18 3 C6
Meadow La MK10 18 D6
Meadow Row MK18 3 B3
Meadow Vw,
 Milton Keynes MK7 36 D1
Meadow Vw,
 Towcester NN12 8 A1
Meadow Walk MK18 3 B3
Meadow Way LU7 39 H2
Meadowsweet MK7 25 F6
Meads Cl MK13 16 B1
Meadway,
 Buckingham MK18 3 C6
Meadway,
 Leighton Buzzard LU7 39 G1
Medale Rd MK6 23 G6
Medeswell MK4 29 E1
Medhurst MK8 21 G3
Medland MK6 24 B4
Medway Cl MK16 14 B3
Melbourne Ter MK13 16 A1
Melfort Dr,
 Leighton Buzzard LU7 38 A3
Melfort Dr,
 Milton Keynes MK2 34 A3
Melick Rd MK6 23 G6
Mellish Cl MK3 29 F2
Melrose Av MK3 29 F3
Melton MK14 16 C1
Melville St MK9 17 G4
Mendelssohn Gro MK7 25 F6
Mentieth Cl MK4 34 A1
Mentmore Ct MK8 21 H5
Mentmore Gdns LU7 38 C4
Mentmore Rd LU7 38 C5
Mentone Av MK4 36 D3
Menzies Cl MK5 22 B6
Mercers Dr MK13 16 B2
Merchant Pl MK10 18 C6
Mercury Gro MK8 26 F1
Meriland Ct MK2 34 B3
Merlewood Dr MK5 28 C1
Merlins Ct LU7 39 E2
Mersey Cl MK3 29 E4
Mersey Way MK3 29 E4
Merthen Gro MK4 28 B5
Merton Dr MK6 23 G6
Metcalfe Gro MK14 13 G5
Michigan Dr MK15 14 A6
Mickleton MK15 17 G2
Middle Grn LU7 39 G2
Middle Slade MK18 3 B6
Middlefield Cl MK4 3 C3
Middlesex Dr MK3 29 F4
Middleton MK14 17 E1
Middleton Way LU7 39 H5
Midsummer Arc MK9 5 E3
Midsummer Blvd MK9 4 B6
Midsummer Pl MK9 5 F3
Midway LU7 39 G3
Mikern Cl MK2 30 A4
Milburn Av MK6 23 E2
Milebush LU7 38 B1
Milecastle MK13 16 A4
Miles Av LU7 39 F2
Miles Cl MK13 13 G4
Milesmere MK8 21 F4
Miletree Ct LU7 39 F1
Milford Av MK11 20 A1
Mill Cl MK12 10 C6
Mill Ho MK16 14 A2
Mill La, Bradville MK13 16 A2
Mill La,
 Buckingham MK18 3 B4
Mill La,
 Old Stratford MK11 9 F6
Mill La,
 Water Eaton MK1 34 C4
Mill La,
 Woburn Sands MK17 36 C2
Mill La, Woolstone MK15 18 A6
Mill Rd,
 Leighton Buzzard LU7 39 E2
Mill Rd,
 Milton Keynes MK2 30 B6
Mill Sq MK12 10 C6
Mill St MK16 14 A2
Mill Way MK17 36 C2

Millbank LU7 38 D2
Millbank Pl MK7 25 E2
Millers Cl LU7 39 H2
Millers Way MK11 20 D2
Millhayes MK14 13 F6
Millholm Rise MK6 24 B6
Millington Gate MK15 18 A1
Millstream Way LU7 38 D2
Milton Dr MK16 14 C2
Milton Gro MK3 29 F6
Milton Keynes General
 Hospital MK6 23 H4
Milton Rd,
 Broughton MK10 19 E6
Milton Rd, Walton MK7 24 D4
Milton Rd, Willen MK15 18 B1
Minerva Gdns MK7 25 G4
Minorca Gro MK5 28 A1
Minshull Cl MK18 3 B3
Minstrel Ct MK13 16 B1
Minton Cl MK14 13 G5
Mitcham Pl MK13 4 B1
Mithras Gdns MK5 25 G5
Mitre Cl MK18 3 A5
Mitre St MK18 3 A5
Moeran Cl MK7 25 F6
Monellan Gro MK7 30 D1
Monks Way MK8 21 E3
Monmouth Gro MK4 27 E6
Monro Av MK8 26 E1
Montagu Dr MK6 23 H3
Montgomery Cl LU7 39 F1
Montgomery Cres MK15 17 G1
Montrose St MK9 17 G4
Moon St MK12 11 G5
Moor Pk MK3 23 G6
Moorend Rd NN12 6 A5
Moorfield MK17 32 D4
Moorfoot MK11 20 D1
Moorgate MK6 23 F4
Moorhen Way MK18 3 C4
Moorhouse Path LU7 39 H5
Moorhouse Way LU7 39 H5
Moors Cl MK18 9 B7
Morar Cl LU7 38 A3
Moray Pl MK3 29 F3
Mordaunts Ct MK15 18 A6
Morebath Gro MK4 28 C1
Moreton Dr MK18 3 C1
Moreton Rd MK18 3 B3
Morland Dr MK8 26 D2
Morley Cres MK7 25 G6
Morrell Cl MK5 22 B5
Morrison Cl MK8 26 E1
Mortain Cl MK7 31 E2
Mortons Fork MK13 11 H5
Mossdale MK13 16 C3
Mount Av MK1 30 B2
Mount Farm
 Ind Est MK1 30 A1
Mount Ho MK1 30 B1
Mount Pleasant,
 Aspley Guise MK17 36 F2
Mount Pleasant,
 Stoke Hammond MK17 7 B5
Mount Pleasant,
 Towcester NN12 6 C5
Mount Pleasant,
 Walton MK6 24 B6
Mount Pleasant Cl MK18 3 A5
Mountbatten Gdns LU7 39 F1
Mounthill Av MK19 9 E5
Mountsfield Cl MK16 14 A4
Mowbray Dr LU7 38 B2
Mozart Cl MK7 31 G1
Muddiford La MK4 28 D1
Muirfield Dr MK3 29 F6
Mullen Av MK14 17 F4
Mullion Pl MK6 23 G2
Murrey Cl MK5 22 C6
Mursley Cl MK11 10 B6
Musgrove Pl MK5 26 F2
Myrtle Bank MK12 21 G1

Nairn Cl MK3 29 E3
Naisby Dr MK17 35 F6
Naphill Pl MK13 4 B1
Napier Cl MK2 30 B4
Napier St MK2 30 B4
Narrow Path MK17 36 B4
Naseby Cl,
 Buckingham MK18 3 C2
Naseby Ct,
 Milton Keynes MK13 16 B2
Nash Cft MK4 28 B5
Nash Rd MK17 27 A6
Nathanial Cl MK6 22 B6
Neapland MK6 23 H6
Neath Cres MK3 29 G3
Nebular Ct LU7 39 G2
Nelson Cl MK8 26 E1
Nelson Ct MK18 3 A4
Nelson Rd LU7 39 F1
Nelson St MK18 3 A4
Nene Cl MK16 14 B3
Nene Dr MK3 29 E4
Neptune Gdns LU7 39 H2

Ness Way MK2 34 B
Nether Gro MK5 28 B
Netley Ct MK5 24 D
Nettlecombe MK4 28 C
Nettleton Cl LU7 39 G
Nevill Cl MK9 7 C
Nevis Cl LU7 38 A
Nevis Gro MK2 34 B
New Rd,
 Leighton Buzzard LU7 38 C
New Rd,
 Milton Keynes MK19 6 C
New St MK11 10 A
Newark Ct MK7 31 E
Newbolt Cl MK16 13 F
Newbridge Oval MK4 28 B
Newbury Ct MK3 32 D
Newby Pl MK4 28 B
Newlyn Pl MK6 23 G
Newman Way LU7 39 F
Newmans Cl MK14 13 F
Newmarket Ct MK10 25 F
Newport Rd,
 Broughton MK16 19 G
Newport Rd,
 Hanslope MK19 7 C
Newport Rd,
 Moulsoe MK16 19 F
Newport Rd,
 New Bradwell MK13 11 G
Newport Rd,
 Willen MK15 18 B
Newport Rd,
 Woburn Sands MK17 36 A
Newport Rd,
 Woolstone MK15 18 A
Woughton on the Green
 MK6,15 24 A
Newton Rd,
 Bletchley MK3 33 E
Newton Rd,
 Newton Longville
 MK17 32 D
Newton Rd,
 Stoke Hammond MK17 7 A
Newton Rd,
 Water Eaton MK17 33 H
Newton Way LU7 39 G
Nicholas Mead MK14 17 F
Nicholson Gro MK8 26 E
Nicolson Dr LU7 39 H
Nielson Ct MK7 25 G
Nightingale Cres MK13 16 A
Nightingale Ho MK7 24 D
Nightingale Pl MK18 3 C
Nixons Cl MK6 23 E
Noble Cl MK15 17 G
Noon Layer Dr MK10 18 B
Norbrek MK8 21 G
Norfolk Ho MK9 4 B
Norman Cres MK10 18 C
Norman Ho MK9 4 B
Normandy Way MK3 29 E
North Crawley Rd MK16 14 C
North Eighth St MK9 4 D
North Eleventh St MK9 17 E
North Fifth St MK9 4 C
North Fourteenth St MK9 17 F
North Fourth St MK9 4 C
North Gate MK2 30 A
North Grafton MK9,13 4 A
North La MK7 24 D
North Ninth St MK9 5 E
North Ridge MK6 23 H
North Row MK9 4 A
North Saxon MK13 4 A
North Second St MK9 4 B
North Seventh St MK9 4 D
North Sixth St MK9 4 C
North Sq MK16 14 B
North St,
 Castlethorpe MK19 6 B
North St,
 Fenny Stratford MK2 30 A
North St,
 Leighton Buzzard LU7 39 E
North Star Dr LU7 39 G
North Tenth St MK9 5 E
North Third St MK9 4 B
North Thirteenth St MK9 17 F
North Twelfth St MK9 17 E
North Way,
 Milton Keynes MK9 9 A
North Way,
 Towcester NN12 8 A
Northampton Rd,
 Milton Keynes MK19 8 E
Northampton Rd,
 Newport Pagnell MK16 14 B
Northampton Rd,
 Towcester NN12 6 C
Northcliffe Cl LU7 39 E
Northcroft MK5 22 B
Northcott MK8 3 B
Northfield Dr MK15 18 C
Northgate Ho MK9 16 E

orthleigh MK4 28 D3
orthwich MK6 24 B4
orton Leys MK7 25 G4
orwood La MK16 13 H3
ottingham Gro MK3 29 E3
ova Lodge MK4 28 B3
ovello Cft MK7 25 G6
uneham Gro MK4 26 F4
ursery Gdns MK13 16 A5
utmeg Cl MK7 25 F6

ak Bank Dr LU7 37 C4
ak Cl LU7 38 B1
ak Ct MK9 5 E3
ak Ho MK4 16 C3
aken Head MK4 28 C3
akham Rise MK4 27 E6
akhill Cl MK5 26 F2
akhill Pk MK5 26 F2
akley Gdns MK15 17 G3
akley Grn LU7 39 F1
akridge MK4 29 E1
akridge Pk LU7 39 F5
aktree Ct MK15 18 A1
akwood Dr MK2 30 B6
atfield Gdns LU7 39 H2
ctavian Dr MK13 21 H1
dell Cl MK6 24 A2
d Belle Ct MK17 7 B5
d Chapel Mews LU7 39 E3
d Groveway MK6 24 B6
d Linslade Rd LU7 37 A5
d Manor Cl MK17 27 B6
d Rd LU7 38 C3
d School Ct,
Buckingham MK18 3 A4
d School Ct,
Leighton Buzzard LU7 39 E2
d Wolverton Rd MK12 10 D5
dbrook Blvd MK6 5 F6
dcastle Cft MK4 28 A4
de Bell La MK5 22 A3
liver Rd MK2 29 H5
mega Ct LU7 39 G2
nslow Ct MK7 31 E1
pal Dr MK15 18 C5
rbison Ct MK8 21 G6
rchard Cl,
Bletchley MK2 29 F6
rchard Cl,
Newton Longville MK17 32 C4
rchard Cl,
Towcester NN12 6 C5
rchard Dene MK18 3 B2
rchard Dr LU7 38 C4
rford Ct MK5 22 B5
riel Cl MK12 11 E5
rion Way LU7 39 H2
rkney Cl MK3 29 F3
rmonde MK14 16 D2
rmsgill Ct MK13 16 B4
rne Gdns MK15 17 G1
rpington Gro MK5 28 B1
rtensia Dr MK7 25 G3
rwell Cl MK16 13 F2
sborne St,
Bletchley MK2 29 H6
sborne St,
Wolverton MK12 11 F5
sier La MK5 22 B6
sier Way MK18 3 B6
sprey Cl MK6 23 G3
sprey Walk MK18 3 D5
stlers La MK11 10 A5
sville Ct MK5 28 D4
tters Brook MK18 3 C5
usebank St MK16 14 B2
usebank Way MK11 10 A6
uzel Cl MK3 29 E4
verend Cl MK13 16 A5
vergate MK9 17 G4
vern Av MK18 3 A3
vern Cl MK18 3 B3
vern Cres MK18 3 A3
versley Ct MK14 13 F6
verstreet MK15 17 F1
ville Ct MK5 22 B5
xendon Ct LU7 37 B5
xfield Park Dr MK19 9 F5
xford Cl,
Fenny Stratford MK2 30 A5
xford St,
Stony Stratford MK11 10 A6
xford St,
Wolverton MK12 11 F5
xhouse Ct MK5 28 A2
xman La MK12 10 D6
xwich Gro MK4 28 B5

addock Cl MK14 17 E1
addock Way MK4 30 B4
adstow Av MK6 5 G4
age Hill Av MK18 3 C3
age's Ind Pk LU7 39 F5
agg's Ct LU7 14 A2
alace Sq MK6 23 F4
almer Cres LU7 39 H4

Pannier Pl MK14 17 G3
Paprika Ct MK7 25 F6
Paradise MK17 32 D3
Park Av MK16 13 H3
Park Cl MK19 10 B1
Park Gdns MK3 29 G4
Park House Dr MK5 26 F1
Park Mews LU7 39 F4
Park Rd, Hanslope MK19 7 C2
Park Rd,
Stony Stratford MK11 20 A1
Park View Ct LU7 38 C3
Park Vw MK16 14 B2
Parker Cl MK13 16 A2
Parklands MK14 12 D6
Parkminster MK10 24 D1
Parkside MK4 29 E1
Parkway,
Bow Brickhill MK17 31 G3
Parkway,
Woburn Sands MK17 36 A1
Parneleys MK10 18 D6
Parrock La MK10 18 D6
Parsley Cl MK7 25 E5
Parsons Cl LU7 39 E4
Parsons Cres MK5 22 C6
Partridge Cl MK18 3 D5
Pascal Dr MK5 26 E2
Passalewe La MK7 25 G4
Passenham La MK19 9 D7
Passmore MK6 24 A4
Pastern Pl MK14 17 F4
Patricks La MK19 9 B8
Patriot Dr MK13 22 B1
Pattison La MK15 18 A6
Paxton Cres MK5 22 B6
Payne's Ct MK18 3 B3
Paynes Dr MK5 22 A3
Peacock Hay MK4 28 C3
Peacock Mews LU7 39 E4
Peacock Yd LU7 39 E3
Pear Tree La MK6 23 F5
Pearse Gro MK7 25 E6
Peartree La LU7 39 E2
Peckover Ct MK8 21 H4
Peebles Pl MK3 29 F2
Peel Ct LU7 39 F2
Peel Rd MK12 11 F5
Peers Dr MK17 36 E3
Peers St MK5 22 B5
Pegasus Rd LU7 39 G2
Pelham Pl MK14 17 F4
Pelton Ct MK5 22 C5
Pembridge Gro MK4 27 E6
Pencarrow Pl MK6 5 H4
Pendennis Ct MK4 28 A5
Pengelly Ct MK6 5 H6
Penhale Cl MK4 28 B4
Penina Cl MK3 28 D4
Penlee Rise MK4 28 B5
Penley Way LU7 39 E4
Penn Rd MK2 30 C4
Pennivale Cl LU7 39 E1
Pennycress Way MK16 13 F2
Pennycuik MK17 35 G6
Pennyroyal MK7 25 E4
Penryn Av MK16 5 H5
Pentewan Gate MK6 5 G4
Pentlands MK11 20 C1
Percheron Pl MK14 17 F4
Peregrine Cl MK6 23 G3
Permayne MK13 16 A1
Perracombe MK4 29 E2
Perran Av MK6 5 H6
Pershore Cft MK10 25 E1
Perth Cl MK3 29 F2
Peterborough Gate
MK15 17 H2
Petersham Cl MK14 14 A4
Pettingrew Cl MK7 25 E5
Petworth MK8 21 G5
Petworth Ho MK8 21 H5
Pevensey Cl MK4 29 E6
Peverel Dr MK1 29 G1
Phillimore Cl MK14 17 H2
Phillip Ct MK5 22 B5
Phoebe La MK17 25 H6
Phoebe's Orch MK17 7 C5
Phoenix Cl LU7 39 H1
Phoenix Dr MK6 23 E4
Pickering Dr MK4 28 B2
Picton St MK16 27 E6
Pightle Cres MK18 3 B2
Pigott Dr MK5 22 A5
Pilgrim St MK9 17 G4
Pimpernel Gro MK7 25 E4
Pinders Cft MK12 21 E1
Pine Cl LU7 37 C5
Pine Crest Mews LU7 38 C3
Pine Gro MK17 11 H2
Pinewood Dr MK2 30 B6
Pinfold MK7 25 H6
Pinkard Ct MK6 24 A3
Pinkle Hill Rd LU7 37 A5
Pinks Cl MK5 22 C3
Pinkworthy MK4 28 B5
Pipard MK14 17 E1
Pippin Cl MK16 13 G3

Pipston Grn MK7 25 E4
Pitcher La MK5 22 B2
Pitchford Av MK18 3 C2
Pitchford Walk MK18 3 C3
Pitfield MK11 20 D2
Pitt Grn MK18 3 D3
Plantain Ct MK7 25 E4
Plantation Pl MK5 28 A1
Plantation Rd LU7 37 A4
Pleshey Cl MK5 22 B4
Plover Cl,
Buckingham MK18 3 C6
Plover Cl,
Newport Pagnell MK16 14 D4
Plowman Cl MK12 21 E1
Plum Tree La LU7 39 E2
Plumstead Av MK13 4 C1
Plymouth Gro MK4 28 B4
Pollys Yd MK16 14 B2
Polmartin Ct MK6 5 H6
Polruan Pl MK6 5 H5
Pomander Cres MK7 25 F4
Pond Cl MK7 32 C5
Pondgate MK7 25 E3
Poplar Cl,
Leighton Buzzard LU7 37 C6
Poplar Cl,
Milton Keynes MK6 24 B6
Poplars Rd MK18 3 B4
Porlock La MK4 28 C1
Portchester Ct MK8 21 H5
Porter's Cl MK19 9 B7
Portfield Cl MK18 3 C4
Portfield Way MK18 3 C4
Portfields Rd MK16 13 G3
Porthcawl Grn MK4 28 C5
Porthleven Pl MK6 5 H3
Porthmellin Cl MK4 28 B5
Portishead Dr,
Milton Keynes MK4 27 F7
Portishead Dr,
Milton Keynes MK4 27 F6
Portland Dr MK15 18 A1
Portmarnock Cl MK3 28 C4
Portrush Cl MK3 28 D5
Portway,
Grange Farm MK5 26 D2
Portway,
Milton Keynes MK9 4 A3
Potters La MK11 21 E2
Pound Hill MK17 35 G6
Poundfield Rd NN12 8 B2
Powell Haven MK10 18 B6
Powis La MK4 27 F5
Precedent Dr MK13 16 B6
Prentice Gro MK5 28 B2
Presley Way MK8 21 G6
Prestwick Cl MK4 28 D6
Primrose Rd MK13 16 A5
Primrose Way MK18 3 A5
Princes Cl LU7 39 E2
Princes Ct LU7 39 E2
Princes Way MK2 29 H4
Priors Pk MK4 28 D3
Priory Cl MK16 14 B2
Priory St MK16 14 B2
Pritchard Ct MK14 13 E6
Prospect Ct NN12 6 C5
Prospect Pl MK19 6 B2
Prospect Rd MK11 9 F6
Protheroe Fld MK7 31 G1
Providence Pl MK13 16 A5
Pulborough Cl MK3 28 D4
Pulford Rd LU7 39 E3
Purbeck MK14 16 C2
Purcel Dr MK16 13 H3
Purwell Walk LU7 37 D4
Putman Ho MK5 22 C5
Puxley Rd,
Deanshanger MK19 9 A7
Puxley Rd,
Old Stratford MK19 9 C7
Pyke Hayes MK8 21 G2
Pyxe Ct MK7 25 E6

Quadrans Cl MK15 17 G1
Quantock Cres MK4 28 D3
Queen Anne St MK13 11 H4
Queen Eleanor St MK11 9 F6
Queen St,
Leighton Buzzard LU7 39 E2
Queen St,
Stony Stratford MK11 10 B5
Queens Av MK16 14 A2
Queens Cl MK9 5 E2
Queensway MK2 30 A5
Quilter Mdw MK7 25 H6
Quince Cl MK7 25 F5
Quinton Dr MK13 16 B6

Rackstraw Gro MK7 25 H6
Radcliffe St,
Milton Keynes MK12 11 F5
Radcliffe St,
Milton Keynes MK12 11 F4
Radian Ct MK5 22 C4
Radman Gro MK12 10 D6
Radworthy MK4 28 C1

Raglan Dr MK4 27 E6
Rainbow Dr,
Milton Keynes MK6 23 F4
Rainbow Dr,
Milton Keynes MK6 23 F3
Rainsborough MK14 13 G6
Ramsay Cl MK13 16 B5
Ramsgill Ct MK13 16 C4
Ramsons Av MK14 17 E5
Ramsthorn Gro MK7 25 E4
Randolph Cl MK13 16 A3
Ranelagh Gdns MK16 14 A4
Rangers Ct MK8 21 H5
Rannoch Ct MK2 34 B1
Rannock Gdns LU7 38 A3
Rashleigh Pl MK13 23 E3
Rathbone Cl MK8 21 G6
Ravel Ct MK7 25 G5
Ravenglass Cft MK10 19 E6
Ravensbourne Pl MK7 17 H6
Ravenscar Ct MK4 28 C3
Ravenstone Ho MK16 19 F5
Ravigill Pl MK12 21 F1
Rawlins Rd MK13 16 A4
Rayleigh Cl MK5 22 B5
Reach Grn LU7 37 C1
Reach La LU7 37 C3
Rectory Flds MK15 18 A6
Red House Cl MK17 32 D3
Red Lion Ct LU7 37 C2
Redbourne Ct MK11 20 C1
Redbridge MK14 16 D1
Redcote Manor MK7 30 D1
Redding Gro MK8 26 E1
Redhuish Cl MK4 28 D1
Redland Dr MK5 22 C3
Redshaw Cl MK18 3 C3
Redvers Gate MK15 17 H1
Redwing Ho MK7 24 D2
Redwood Gate MK5 22 C6
Redwood Glade LU7 37 B5
Reeves Cft MK12 21 F1
Regency Ct MK9 4 C3
Regent St,
Leighton Buzzard LU7 39 F2
Regent St,
Stony Stratford MK2 30 A5
Regus Ho MK10 18 D4
Reliance La MK8 17 H5
Rendlesham MK15 18 A6
Renny Park Rd MK16 14 C4
Reynolds Pl MK8 26 E1
Rhodes Pl MK8 23 E3
Rhondda Cl MK1 30 B3
Rhoscolyn Dr MK4 28 C5
Rhuddlan Cl MK5 22 A4
Ribble Cl MK16 14 B3
Ribble Cres MK3 28 D4
Richardson Pl MK6 5 E6
Richborough MK13 16 A3
Richmond Cl MK3 28 D3
Richmond Rd LU7 39 G4
Richmond Way MK16 14 A3
Rickley La MK3 29 F4
Rickyard Cl MK13 16 A5
Ridgeway,
Stony Stratford MK11 20 B2
Ridgeway,
Wolverton Mill East
MK12 10 D6
Ridgmont MK19 9 A7
Ridgmont Cl MK19 9 A7
Ridgway MK17 36 B1
Rillington Gdns MK4 28 B2
Rimsdale Ct MK2 34 A3
Ring East MK7 24 D4
Ring Rd North MK7 24 C4
Ring Rd West MK7 24 C4
River Cl MK16 14 A3
Rivercrest Rd MK19 9 E5
Riverside,
Leighton Buzzard LU7 39 E1
Riverside,
Newport Pagnell MK16 14 B2
Rixband Cl MK7 31 E1
Roberts Cl MK19 9 B8
Robertson Cl MK15 21 H6
Robin Cl MK18 3 D5
Robins Hill MK6 23 G5
Robinswood Cl LU7 37 B5
Roche Gdns MK3 29 G4
Rochester Cl MK5 22 B6
Rochester Mews LU7 38 C3
Rochfords MK6 23 F4
Rock Cl LU7 38 B3
Rock La LU7 38 B3
Rockingham Dr MK14 17 E3
Rockleigh Ct LU7 38 C2
Rockspray Gro MK7 25 E5
Rodwell Gdns MK7 31 G1
Roebuck Way MK5 22 C5
Roeburn Cres MK4 28 C4
Rogers Cft MK6 24 B4
Rolvenden Gro MK7 25 F5
Romar Ct MK1 30 A3
Roosevelt Av LU7 39 F1
Ropa Ct LU7 38 D3
Rosebay Cl MK7 25 F6

Rosebery Av LU7 38 C3
Rosebery Ct LU7 38 D3
Rosecomb Pl MK5 22 B6
Rosemullion Av MK4 28 B5
Roslyn Ct MK15 18 B1
Ross Way MK3 29 F2
Rossal Pl MK12 21 F1
Rossendale MK14 16 D1
Rossini Pl MK7 25 G5
Rothersthorpe MK14 17 G1
Rothschild Rd LU7 38 C1
Rotten Row MK17 35 F5
Roundel Dr LU7 39 G4
Routeco
Retail Pk MK6 22 D3
Roveley Ct MK11 20 B1
Rowan Dr MK19 11 G1
Rowlands Cl MK2 30 B5
Rowle Cl MK14 17 E2
Rowley Furrows LU7 38 C1
Rowsham Dell MK14 13 F4
Roxburgh Way MK3 29 F2
Rubbra Cl MK7 25 G5
Rudchesters MK13 16 A4
Rumbold's St MK18 3 B4
Runford Ct MK5 22 C5
Runnymede MK14 13 F5
Rushleys Cl MK5 22 A3
Rushmere Cl MK7 31 G3
Rushmere
Retail Pk MK1 30 A3
Rushton Ct MK8 21 H5
Ruskin Ct MK16 14 A4
Rusland Circus MK4 28 C3
Russell St,
Stony Stratford MK11 10 A6
Russell St,
Woburn Sands MK17 36 B3
Russell Way LU7 39 G3
Rutherford Gate MK5 22 C6
Ruthven Cl MK4 34 A3
Rycroft MK4 28 B5
Rydal Way MK2 34 B1
Rye Cl LU7 39 H2
Ryeland MK11 10 B5
Rylands Mews LU7 39 E3
Rylstone Cl MK13 16 B5
Ryton Pl MK4 28 C2

Saddlers Pl MK14 17 G3
Sadleirs Grn MK17 36 B2
Saffron St MK2 30 A6
St Aidan's Cl MK3 33 E1
St Andrews Cl LU7 39 F2
St Andrew's Ho MK7 30 D3
St Andrew's Rd MK3 29 E6
St Andrew's St LU7 39 E2
St Anne's Ho MK7 30 D3
St Anthonys Pl MK4 28 B5
St Bartholomews MK10 24 D2
St Bees MK10 25 E1
St Botolphs MK10 25 E2
St Brides Cl MK6 17 H6
St Catherine's Av MK3 32 D1
St Clement's Dr MK3 28 D6
St David's Rd MK3 33 E1
St Dunstans MK6 23 G4
St Edwards Ct MK14 17 F2
St Faith's Cl MK17 32 D4
St George's Cl LU7 39 F2
St George's Ct LU7 39 F2
St George's Ho MK7 30 D3
St George's Rd MK3 28 D6
St Georges Way MK12 11 G4
St Giles St MK13 11 H4
St Govans Cl MK4 28 C5
St Helens Gro MK10 24 D2
St Ives Cres MK4 28 B5
St James Cl MK19 7 B2
St James St MK13 11 H4
St John St MK16 14 A2
St John's Cl MK12 11 F6
St John's Rd MK3 32 D1
St Johns Ter MK16 14 B2
St Lawrence Vw MK13 16 A5
St Leger Cl MK14 17 E1
St Leger Dr MK14 12 D6
St Leonard's Cl LU7 37 C4
St Margaret Ct MK2 30 B5
St Margarets Cl MK16 14 B3
St Martin's St MK2 30 A5
St Mary St MK13 11 H4
St Mary's Av,
Bletchley MK3 29 E6
St Mary's Av,
Stony Stratford MK11 10 A6
St Mary's Cl MK17 25 H4
St Mary's Ct LU7 38 C2
St Mary's Way LU7 38 C2
St Matthews Ct MK3 33 E1
St Michaels Dr MK7 24 C4
St Patrick's Way MK3 29 E6
St Paul's Ct MK16 9 F6
St Paul's Rd MK3 33 E1
St Pauls Yd MK16 14 A3
St Peters Way MK13 16 A1
St Stephens Dr MK15 17 H1
St Thomas Ct MK4 28 A4

St Vincents MK17 36 C3
Salden Cl MK15 22 B5
Salford Rd MK17 36 D1
Salisbury Gro MK14 13 F5
Salters Mews MK14 17 F2
Salton Link MK4 28 B3
Saltwood Av MK4 27 E6
Samphire Ct MK7 25 E5
San Remo Rd MK17 36 F3
Sandal Ct MK5 22 B5
Sandbrier Cl MK7 25 E5
Sanders La NN12 8 A1
Sandfield Ho LU7 37 D3
Sandhills LU7 39 F1
Sandhurst Dr MK18 3 A5
Sandown Ct MK3 32 D1
Sandringham Ct MK16 13 H3
Sandringham Pl MK2 30 A5
Sandwell Ct MK8 21 E4
Sandy Cl,
  Buckingham MK18 3 D4
Sandy Cl,
  Milton Keynes MK14 12 D6
Sandy La,
  Leighton Buzzard LU7 37 C4
Sandy La,
  Milton Keynes MK19 14 B3
Sandywell Dr MK15 17 G3
Santen Gro MK2 34 B2
Saracens Wharf MK2 30 C4
Saturn Cl LU7 39 H1
Savage Cft MK10 18 C5
Savoy Cres MK9 5 G2
Saxon Ct MK9 5 F4
Saxon Gate MK9 4 D2
Saxon St MK6 5 F5
Saxons Cl LU7 39 G2
Scardale MK13 16 C3
Scatterill Cl MK18 16 B4
School Dr MK17 32 C4
School La,
  Buckingham MK18 3 B3
School La,
  Castlethorpe MK19 6 C2
School La,
  Loughton MK5 22 B3
School La,
  Milton Keynes MK17 7 B4
School La,
  Yardley Gobin NN12 14 B1
School St MK13 16 A1
Schumann Ct MK7 31 G1
Scotney Gdns MK3 29 E5
Scott Dr MK16 13 G2
Scotts Cl MK17 7 B4
Scotts La MK18 3 C1
Scriven Ct MK15 18 B2
Seabrooke Ct MK8 26 E1
Seagrave Ct MK7 24 D6
Secklow Gate MK9 5 F1
Second Av MK1 29 H3
Sedgemere MK8 21 F4
Selbourne Av MK3 29 F6
Selby Gro MK5 22 A6
Selkirk Gro MK3 29 F2
Selworthy MK4 28 D1
Serjeants Grn MK14 17 F2
Serles Cl MK6 23 G5
Serpentine Ct MK4 34 A2
Severn Dr MK16 14 B3
Severn Walk LU7 37 D4
Severn Way MK3 28 D4
Shackleton Pl MK6 5 F5
Shaftesbury Cres MK3 29 G3
Shakespeare Cl MK16 13 F1
Shallowford Gro MK4 28 D1
Shamrock Cl MK7 25 F4
Shannon Ct MK14 17 G3
Sharkham Ct MK4 28 B4
Sharman Walk MK13 16 A5
Shaw Cl MK16 13 F2
Shearmans MK11 20 D2
Sheelin Gro MK2 34 B3
Sheepcoat Cl MK5 22 A6
Sheepcote Cres LU7 37 C2
Sheerness Ct MK4 28 A4
Sheldon Ct MK8 21 H4
Shelley Cl MK16 13 G2
Shelley Dr MK3 29 F6
Shelsmore MK14 17 G1
Shelton Ct MK17 36 B3
Shenley Cl LU7 37 C4
Shenley Hill Rd LU7 37 C4
Shenley Rd,
  Bletchley MK3 29 E3
Shenley Rd,
  Shenley Church End
  MK5 22 A5
Shenley Rd,
  Whaddon MK17 27 C7
Shepherds MK11 20 D1
Shepherds Mead LU7 37 C6
Sheppards Cft MK16 13 H3
Sheppards Grn MK5 26 F1
Shepperton Cl MK19 6 B3
Sherbourne Dr MK7 31 E1
Sherbourne Ho MK7 31 F1
Sherington Rd MK16 14 B1

Shernfold MK7 25 E4
Sherwood Dr MK3 29 G4
Sherwood Ho MK3 29 G4
Shilling Cl MK15 17 G2
Ship Rd LU7 38 C3
Shipley Rd MK16 13 G3
Shipman Ct MK15 17 H2
Shipton Hill MK13 16 B3
Shirley Moor MK7 25 E3
Shirwell Cres MK4 22 D6
Shorham Rise MK8 21 G3
Shouler Cl MK5 22 B6
Shrewsbury Cl MK10 24 D1
Shropshire Ct MK8 29 E3
Shuttleworth Gro MK7 25 G5
Sidlaw Ct MK11 20 C1
Silbury Arc MK9 5 E2
Silbury Blvd MK9 4 A5
Silbury Ct MK9 4 D3
Silicon Ct MK5 22 C5
Silver St,
  Milton Keynes MK11 10 A6
Silver St,
  Newport Pagnell MK16 14 A3
Silverweed Ct MK7 25 E5
Simms Cft MK10 19 E6
Simnel MK6 23 H5
Simons Lea MK5 16 B5
Simonsbath MK4 28 B3
Simpson Dr MK6 24 C5
Simpson Rd MK6,7 24 B5
Sinclair Ct MK4 29 G2
Singleton Dr MK8 26 D2
Sipthorp Cl MK7 25 F5
Sissinghurst Dr MK4 27 F5
Sitwell Ct MK16 13 F1
Skeats Wharf MK15 17 G2
Skeldon Gate MK9 17 G4
Skene Cl MK2 34 A3
Skipton Cl MK15 17 H2
Slade La MK11 20 C1
Slated Row MK12 10 D4
Smabridge Walk MK15 18 B1
Small Cres MK18 3 D4
Smarden Bell MK7 25 E3
Smeaton Cl MK14 13 G5
Smithergill Ct MK13 16 C4
Smithsons Pl MK9 17 G5
Snaith Cres MK5 22 B3
Snelshall St MK4 27 F6
Snowberry Cl MK12 21 F1
Snowdon Dr MK6 22 D3
Snowshill Ct MK14 13 F5
Sokeman Cl MK12 10 D6
Solar Ct MK14 13 E6
Solstice Ho MK9 4 C4
Somerset Cl MK3 29 F3
Sorensen Ct MK5 26 E3
Sorrell Dr MK16 13 F2
Soskin Dr MK14 16 C2
Soulbury Rd LU7 38 A1
South Eighth St MK9 5 F4
South Fifth St MK9 5 E5
South Fourth St MK9 4 D5
South Hall MK18 3 C1
South Ho MK1 30 B2
South Lawne MK3 29 F5
South Ninth St MK9 5 F3
South Row MK9 4 D6
South Second St MK9 4 C6
South Seventh St MK9 5 E4
South Sixth St MK9 5 E4
South St,
  Leighton Buzzard LU7 39 F3
South St,
  Milton Keynes MK19 6 B2
South Tenth St MK9 5 F3
South Ter MK2 29 H5
Southbridge Gro MK7 25 E3
Southcott Village LU7 38 B4
Southcourt Av LU7 38 B3
Southcourt Rd LU7 38 B3
Southern Way MK12 11 F6
Southfield Cl MK15 18 B1
Southgate Ho MK9 5 E3
Southwick Ct MK8 21 H5
Sovereign Cl MK9 4 D4
Sovereign Dr MK15 17 F2
Spark Way MK16 13 F2
Sparsholt Ct MK4 28 C2
Spearmint Cl MK7 25 F6
Specklands MK5 22 A3
Speedwell Pl MK14 17 E5
Speldhurst Ct MK4 28 C3
Spencer MK14 16 C1
Spenlows Rd MK3 29 G2
Spinney Ct LU7 37 C3
Spinney La MK17 36 E3
Spooney Wood MK13 11 H6
Spring Gdns MK16 14 A3
Spring Gro MK17 36 B2
Springfield Blvd MK6 23 H1
Springfield Ct,
  Leighton Buzzard LU7 38 C2
Springfield Ct,
  Milton Keynes MK6 23 H1

Springfield Gdns MK19 9 A8
Springfield Rd LU7 38 C3
Squires Cl MK6 23 G5
Squirrels Way MK18 3 C5
Stacey Av MK12 11 F5
Stacey Bushes Trading Centre
  MK12 21 G2
Stafford Gro MK5 22 B5
Stagshaw Gro MK4 28 B2
Stainton Dr MK13 16 C5
Stamford Av MK6 23 H1
Stanbridge Ct MK11 20 B1
Stanbridge Rd LU7 39 F4
Stanbridge Road Ter LU7 39 F4
Stanbrook Pl MK10 24 D2
Standing Way MK4 32 A1
Stanier Sq MK2 29 H5
Stanmore Gdns MK16 13 H4
Stanton Av MK13 16 A2
Stanton Gate MK14 16 D1
Stanway Cl MK15 17 H3
Staple Hall Rd MK1 30 B3
Staters Pound MK15 17 G2
Statham Pl MK6 5 G6
Station Rd,
  Bow Brickhill MK17 31 E3
Station Rd,
  Buckingham MK18 3 A5
Station Rd,
  Castlethorpe MK19 6 B3
Station Rd,
  Leighton Buzzard LU7 38 C3
Station Rd,
  Newport Pagnell MK16 14 A3
Station Rd,
  Woburn Sands MK17 36 B2
Station Sq MK9 4 B6
Station Ter,
  Buckingham MK18 3 B5
Station Ter,
  Milton Keynes MK14 13 E5
Stavordale MK10 25 E2
Steeple Cl MK4 28 B5
Steinbeck Cres MK4 28 A6
Stephenson Cl LU7 38 C4
Steppingstone Pl LU7 39 F3
Stevens Fld MK7 25 G5
Stirling Cl MK15 17 G2
Stirling Ho MK3 28 D6
Stock La MK17 27 B6
Stockdale MK13 16 C3
Stocking Green Cl MK19 7 C1
Stockwell La MK17 25 G6
Stoke La MK17 35 F6
Stoke Rd,
  Fenny Stratford MK2 30 B6
Stoke Rd,
  Leighton Buzzard LU7 38 C3
Stoke Rd,
  Newton Longville MK17 32 D4
Stokenchurch Pl MK13 16 C5
Stokesay Ct MK4 27 E5
Stolford Rise MK4 28 B4
Stone Hill MK8 21 G4
Stonecrop Pl MK14 17 E5
Stonegate MK13 16 A3
Stoneleigh Ct MK4 21 H5
Stonor Ct MK8 21 H5
Stotfold Ct MK11 20 B1
Stour Cl,
  Milton Keynes MK3 29 E5
Stour Cl,
  Newport Pagnell MK16 14 C3
Stourhead Gate MK4 27 E5
Stowe Av MK18 3 A2
Stowe Cl MK18 3 A3
Stowe Ct MK14 16 C1
Stowe Rise MK18 3 A3
Strangford Dr MK4 34 A3
Stratford Ct MK8 21 H4
Stratford Arc MK11 10 A6
Stratford Rd,
  Buckingham MK18 3 C3
Stratford Rd,
  Deanshanger MK19 9 B8
Stratford Rd,
  Old Stratford MK19 8 F4
Stratford Rd,
  Whaddon MK17 26 A4
Stratford Rd,
  Wolverton MK12 10 B5
Strathnaver Pl MK12 21 F1
Stratton Mews LU7 39 F3
Strauss Gro MK4 31 G1
Streatham Pl MK13 4 A2
Strudwick Dr MK6 23 E2
Stuart Cl MK2 30 B4
Stubbs Fld MK5 28 A2
Studley Knapp MK7 25 E4
Sturges Cl MK7 24 D6
Sudgrow Ho MK15 17 G3
Sulgrave Cl MK8 21 H5
Sullivan Cres MK7 25 G6
Sultan Cft MK5 28 A1
Summer Cl LU7 39 F2
Summergill Ct MK13 16 C4
Summerhayes MK14 17 E1
Summerson Rd MK6 23 F6

Sumner Ct MK5 22 A3
Sunbury Cl MK13 16 A3
Sunderland Ct MK4 27 F6
Sunningdale Ho MK17 31 E3
Sunningdale Way MK3 28 D5
Sunridge Cl MK16 13 H4
Sunrise Parkway MK14 17 E3
Sunset Cl MK2 30 A6
Surrey Pl MK3 29 F3
Surrey Rd MK3 29 F3
Surrey St MK13 4 B2
Sussex Rd MK3 29 F4
Sutcliffe Av MK6 5 E6
Sutherland Gro MK3 29 F3
Sutleye Ct MK5 22 B6
Sutton Ct MK4 28 C4
Swales Dr LU7 39 H4
Swallow Cl MK18 3 C5
Swallowfield MK8 21 H4
Swan Cl MK18 3 C5
Swan Ct LU7 38 C4
Swanwick La MK10 19 E6
Swayne Rise MK10 25 E1
Sweetlands Cnr MK7 25 E3
Swift Cl MK16 13 G2
Swimbridge La MK4 28 D1
Swinden Ct MK13 16 B4
Sycamore Av MK2 30 B5
Sycamore Cl MK18 3 D5
Sykes Cft MK4 28 C3
Sylvester St LU7 37 C3
Symington Ct MK5 22 C5
Syon Gdns MK16 13 H4

Tabard Gdns MK16 14 A5
Tacknell Dr MK5 28 A1
Tadmarton MK15 17 G3
Tadmere MK8 21 G4
Talbot Ct,
  Leighton Buzzard LU7 39 E1
Talbot Ct,
  Milton Keynes MK15 24 A1
Talland Av MK6 5 G5
Tallis La MK7 25 F6
Tamar Ho MK3 29 E4
Tamar Walk LU7 37 D4
Tamarisk Ct MK7 25 E6
Tamworth Stubb MK7 25 E5
Tandra MK6 23 H4
Tanfield La MK10 18 D5
Tanners Dr MK14 13 G4
Tansman La MK7 25 G6
Taranis Cl MK7 25 E6
Tarbert Cl MK2 34 A2
Tarnbrook Cl MK4 28 B3
Tarragon Cl MK7 25 E5
Tatling Gro MK7 25 F5
Tattam Ct MK15 24 A1
Tattenhoe La MK3 28 D3
Tattenhoe St MK5,8 26 D2
Tattershall Cl MK5 22 A5
Taunton Deane MK4 28 D3
Tavelhurst MK8 21 H4
Taverner Cl MK7 25 G6
Tavistock Cl MK11 36 A1
Tavistock St MK2 30 A4
Tay Rd MK3 29 E4
Taylors Mews MK14 17 F2
Taylor's Ride LU7 37 B6
Taymouth Pl MK9 17 H5
Teasel Av MK14 17 E4
Tees Way MK3 29 E4
Teign Cl MK16 14 B3
Telford Way MK14 13 G5
Temperance Ter MK11 9 F6
Temple Cl,
  Buckingham MK18 3 C2
Temple Cl,
  Milton Keynes MK3 28 D6
Tene Acres MK5 26 F1
Tennyson Dr MK16 13 G3
Tennyson Gro MK3 29 F6
Tenterden Cres MK7 25 E4
Tewkesbury La MK10 24 C2
Thames Cl MK3 29 E5
Thames Dr MK16 14 B3
Thane Ct MK14 16 C1
The Approach MK8 21 G2
The Beeches MK19 9 B8
The Boundary MK6 5 G6
The Canons MK16 14 C3
The Carne MK11 20 C1
the centre :mk MK9 5 F2
The Chequers MK16 6 B2
The Chestnuts MK19 6 B2
The Chilterns LU7 39 G4
The Close,
  Bradville MK13 16 B5
The Close,
  Woburn Sands MK17 36 B2
The Close,
  Woughton on the Green
  MK6 24 B3
The Courtyard MK14 13 E5
The Craven MK13 16 C5
The Crescent,
  Fenny Stratford MK2 30 A4

The Crescent,
  Great Linford MK14 13 E
The Crescent,
  Haversham MK19 11 G
The Dell LU7 37 C
The Don MK3 28 D
The Elms,
  Leighton Buzzard LU7 38 C
The Elms,
  Milton Keynes MK3 29 F
The Fleet MK6 23 H
The Gables LU7 38 C
The Green,
  Cosgrove MK19 10 E
The Green,
  Deanshanger MK19 9 B
The Green,
  Hanslope MK19 7 C
The Green,
  Loughton MK5 22 B
The Green,
  Newport Pagnell MK16 14 A
The Green,
  Stoke Hammond MK17 7 B
The Green,
  Woughton on the Green
  MK6 24 A
The Greys MK6 24 A
The Grove,
  Bletchley MK3 29 H
The Grove,
  Bradwell MK13 16 A
The Grove,
  Newport Pagnell MK16 13 H
The Grove,
  Woburn Sands MK17 36 B
The Heath LU7 37 A
The Hedgerows MK4 29 E
The Hide MK6 23 H
The High St MK8 21 H
The Holt MK5 3 C
The Homestead MK5 22 A
The Hooke MK15 18 E
The Hythe MK8 21 G
The Laurels MK17 30 E
The Leys MK17 36 E
The Limes,
  Fenny Stratford MK2 30 G
The Limes,
  Stony Stratford MK11 20 A
The Linx MK3 29 G
The Lodge Pk MK16 13 H
The Maltings LU7 39 F
The Martins Dr LU7 38 D
The Meadway MK5 22 B
The Mount,
  Aspley Guise MK17 36 D
The Mount,
  Simpson MK6 24 E
The Nortons MK7 31 E
The Oval MK6 23 E
The Paddocks LU7 38 C
The Ridings MK19 9 A
The Ryding MK5 28 A
The Slade MK17 32 D
The Spinney MK13 16 A
The Square,
  Aspley Guise MK17 36 E
The Square,
  Wolverton MK12 11 F
The Stile LU7 37 C
The Stocks MK19 10 B
The Terrace MK17 36 E
The Walnuts LU7 37 C
The Wharf,
  Great Linford MK14 13 E
The Wharf,
  Water Eaton MK2 34 B
The Wood LU7 39 E
Theatre Walk MK9 5 F
Theydon Av MK17 36 D
Third Av MK1 29 H
Thirlby La MK5 22 A
Thirlmere Av MK4 34 A
Thirsk Gdns MK3 32 C
Thomas Dr MK16 13 G
Thomas St LU7 37 C
Thompson St MK13 16 A
Thorncliffe MK8 21 F
Thorneycroft La MK15 17 E
Thornley Cft MK4 28 D
Thornton Rd MK19 20 A
Thorpeness Cft MK4 28 A
Thorwold Pl MK5 22 B
Thresher Gro MK12 10 D
Threshers Ct LU7 39 H
Thrift Rd LU7 37 C
Thrupp Cft MK19 6 C
Thurne Cl MK16 16 B
Thursby Cl MK15 18 B
Thyme Cl MK16 13 F
Ticehurst Ct MK7 25 E
Tickford Arc MK16 14 A
Tickford St MK16 14 A
Tidbury Cl MK17 36 A
Tiffany Cl MK7 25 E
Tilbrook Ind Est MK7 31 F
Tilers Rd MK11 21 E

iller Ct LU7 39 H3
illman Cl MK12 21 E1
im La MK18 3 C4
imberscombe MK4 28 D1
imbold Dr MK7 24 D3
mor Ct MK11 10 A6
ndall Av LU7 39 F1
ngewick Rd MK18 3 A4
ingewick Rd Ind Est MK18 3 A4
intagel Ct MK6 5 H6
ippet Cl MK7 31 G1
itchmarsh Ct MK6 23 E3
iverton Cres MK4 27 E6
olcarne Av MK6 23 G2
ompkins Cl MK5 28 B1
ongwell MK15 14 A6
ongwell La MK16 13 H6
ongwell St MK10,15 18 B1
oombs Yd MK18 3 B3
oot Hill Cl MK5 22 A6
op Mdw MK7 31 E1
orre Cl MK3 29 F3
orridon Ct MK2 34 A3
owan Av MK6 5 H6
owcester Rd MK19 9 E5
ower Cres MK14 17 F2
ower Dr MK14 17 E2
ownsend Gro MK13 16 B1
rafalgar Av MK3 29 E3
ranlands Brigg MK13 16 B5
ravell Ct MK13 16 B5
ravis Gro MK3 29 G5
reborough MK4 28 D2
redington Gro MK7 31 E1
remayne Ct MK6 5 H6
rent Dr MK16 14 B3
rent Rd MK3 29 E4
rent Way LU7 39 H5
rentishoe Cres MK4 28 D2
resham Ct MK5 22 A3
revithick La MK5 22 B6
revone Ct MK6 5 H6
rinity Cl MK19 9 E5
rinity Rd MK12 10 D4
rispen Ct MK6 5 H6
routbeck MK6 23 H2
rubys Gdn MK6 23 G4
rueman Pl MK6 23 F2
rumpton La MK7 25 G4
runk Furlong MK17 36 D1
udeley Hale MK7 25 E3
udor Ct LU7 38 D3
udor Gdns MK11 20 B2
ulla Ct MK2 34 A3
ummell Way MK2 34 A2
unbridge Gro MK7 25 E2
urnberry Cl MK3 28 D6
urnberry Ho MK7 31 E3
urners Mews MK14 17 F2
urneys Dr MK12 10 C5
urnmill Av MK6 17 H6
urnmill Ct MK6 17 H6
urnpike Ct MK17 36 A1
urpyn Ct MK6 24 B3
urvill End MK5 22 B2
weed Dr MK3 28 D4
winflower MK7 25 E5
witchen La MK4 28 D2
wyford La MK7 25 F6
yburn Av MK6 17 H6
ylers Grn MK13 4 C1
yne Sq MK3 28 D4
ynemouth Rise MK10 24 D2
yrell Cl MK18 3 A5
yrells Gdns MK17 7 C4
yrells Rd MK17 7 B4
yrill MK14 16 C2
yson Pl MK6 23 E3

llswater Dr LU7 38 A3
Jlverscroft MK10 25 E1
Jlyett Pl MK6 23 E3
Jnderwood Pl MK6 23 E3
Jnion St MK16 14 A2
Jpper Coombe LU7 38 C1
Jpper Fifth St MK9 4 D3
Jpper Fourth St MK9 4 C4
Jpper Second St MK9 4 B4
Jpper Stonehayes MK14 17 F1
Jpper Third St MK9 4 B4
Jpper Way MK17 35 G5
Jpper Wood Cl MK5 28 A2
Jpton Gro MK5 22 C6

ache La MK5 26 F2
alens Cl MK8 26 E1
alentine Ct MK8 21 G6
alerian Pl MK16 13 F2
alley Rd MK18 3 D3
Van Der Bilt Ct MK13 11 H5
Vandke Mews MK17 36 B1
Vandyke Cl MK17 36 B1
Vandyke Rd LU7 39 F2
Vantage Ct MK16 14 C3
Vauxhall MK13 16 B3
Vellan Av MK6 23 G2
Venables La MK15 17 G1
Verdi Cl MK7 25 G6
Verdon Dr MK15 17 H2
Verity Pl MK6 5 F6
Verley Cl MK6 24 A3
Vermont Pl MK15 14 A6
Verney Cl MK18 3 B3
Vernier Cres MK5 26 E3
Veryan Pl MK6 23 G1
Vicarage Cl NN12 6 B5
Vicarage Ct MK19 7 C2
Vicarage Gdns, Leighton Buzzard LU7 38 C3
Vicarage Gdns, Milton Keynes MK13 16 A5
Vicarage Rd, Bradwell MK13 16 A5
Vicarage Rd, Fenny Stratford MK2 30 B5
Vicarage Rd, Leighton Buzzard LU7 38 C3
Vicarage Rd, Stony Stratford MK11 10 A5
Vicarage Rd, Whaddon MK17 27 B7
Vicarage St MK17 36 C3
Vicarage Walk MK11 10 A6
Victoria Rd, Leighton Buzzard LU7 38 C3
Victoria Rd, Milton Keynes MK2 30 B5
Victoria Row MK18 3 B4
Victoria St MK12 11 F5
Victoria Ter LU7 39 H2
Vienna Gro MK13 11 H5
Village Ct LU7 38 B4
Villiers Cl MK18 3 C2
Vimy Ct LU7 38 D2
Vimy Rd LU7 38 D3
Vincent Av MK8 21 H6
Vintners Mews MK14 17 F2
Virginia MK6 23 G4
Viscount Way MK2 29 H4
Volta Rise MK5 22 C6
Vyne Cres MK8 22 A2

Waddesdon Cl MK8 21 H5
Wadesmill La MK7 31 E1
Wadhurst La MK7 25 E2
Wadworth Holme MK10 18 C5
Wagner Cl MK7 31 F1
Waine Cl MK18 3 B5
Wainers Cft MK12 21 E1
Wakefield Cl MK14 17 F2
Walbank Gro MK5 28 A2
Walbrook Av MK6 17 H6
Walgrave Dr MK13 16 B5
Walkhampton Av MK13 16 C6
Wallace St MK13 11 H4
Wallinger Dr MK5 28 A2
Wallingford MK13 16 B3
Wallmead Gdns MK5 22 B4
Walney Pl MK4 28 A4
Walnut Cl MK16 13 G3
Walnut Dr MK2 30 B5
Walsh's Manor MK14 16 D1
Waltham Dr MK10 25 E2
Walton Dr MK7 24 C4
Walton End MK7 25 G5
Walton Heath MK3 28 D5
Walton Rd, Caldecotte MK7 31 E1
Walton Rd, Milton Keynes Village MK10 18 D6
Walton Rd, Walton MK7 24 D5
Walton Rd, Wavendon Gate MK7 25 G4
Wandlebury MK14 17 G1
Wandsworth Pl MK13 4 C1
Ward Rd MK1 30 B2
Wardle Pl MK6 23 E2
Wardstone End MK4 28 C3
Warmington Gdns MK15 17 H4
Warneford Way LU7 39 G4
Warners Cl MK17 35 G6
Warners Rd MK17 32 D4
Warren Rd NN12 6 C5
Warwick Pl MK3 29 E5
Warwick Rd, Bletchley MK3 29 E5
Warwick Rd, Hanslope MK19 7 C1
Washfield MK4 28 D2
Wastel MK6 23 H5
Watchcroft Dr MK18 3 C2
Watchet Ct MK4 28 D2
Water Cl, Milton Keynes MK19 9 E5
Water Cl, Newport Pagnell MK16 14 C3
Water Eaton Rd MK2,3 29 H5
Water La LU7 38 D3
Waterborne Walk LU7 39 E3
Waterdell LU7 39 G3
Waterford Cl MK3 29 E3
Waterhouse Cl MK16 14 A2
Waterloo Ct MK3 29 E3
Waterloo Rd LU7 38 C3
Waterlow Cl MK16 14 A4
Waterside MK6 23 H2
Waterside Pk MK12 11 E4
Watersmeet Cl MK4 28 D1
Watling St, Fenny Stratford MK1,2 30 A3
Watling St, Kiln Farm MK11 20 D2
Watling St, Towcester NN12 8 A1
Watling Ter MK2 30 C4
Watlow Gdns MK18 3 D2
Watten Ct MK2 34 B3
Watts Cl MK19 7 B1
Wavell Ct MK15 17 G1
Waverley Cft MK10 24 D2
Wealdstone Pl MK6 17 G6
Weasel La MK17 32 B1
Weathercock Cl MK17 36 B2
Weathercock La MK17 36 B2
Weavers End MK19 7 C2
Weavers Hill MK11 20 C2
Webber Heath MK7 31 G1
Webbs Home Cl MK10 19 E6
Websters Mdw MK4 28 C3
Wedgwood Av MK14 13 G5
Welbeck Cl MK10 24 C1
Weldon Rise MK5 22 B3
Well St MK18 3 B4
Welland Dr MK16 14 B3
Welland Ho MK3 29 E5
Wellfield Ct MK15 18 A1
Wellhayes MK14 17 F1
Wellington Ho LU7 37 C3
Wellington Pl MK3 29 H6
Wells Ct LU7 39 E2
Welsummer Gro MK5 28 A2
Wenning La MK4 28 B3
Wentworth Dr LU7 39 E1
Wentworth Way MK3 28 C6
Werth Dr MK17 36 B4
West Ct LU7 39 E3
West Dales MK13 16 C3
West Hill MK17 36 D3
West Rd MK17 36 B2
West St, Buckingham MK18 3 A3
West St, Leighton Buzzard LU7 38 D3
West Walk MK9 5 E3
Westbourne Ct MK13 16 A2
Westbrook End MK17 32 C4
Westbury Cl MK16 13 H2
Westbury La MK16 13 F1
Westcliffe MK8 21 F4
Western Av MK18 3 A3
Western Dr MK19 7 B1
Western Rd, Fenny Stratford MK2 30 A4
Western Rd, Wolverton MK12 11 E5
Westfield Av MK19 9 A7
Westfield Rd MK2 30 A5
Westfields MK18 3 A4
Westhill MK14 16 D1
Westminster Dr MK3 29 F4
Westminster Ho MK9 5 E4
Weston Av LU7 39 G4
Westside LU7 39 E2
Westwood Cl MK8 21 H5
Wetherby Gdns MK3 32 D1
Whaddon Rd, Newport Pagnell MK16 13 H4
Whaddon Rd, Newton Longville MK17 32 C3
Whaddon Rd, Shenley Brook End MK5 28 B2
Whaddon Rd, Westcroft MK4 27 E6
Whaddon Way MK3 28 D6
Whalley Dr MK3 29 F2
Wharf Hill Ter MK18 3 C3
Wharf La MK19 9 E5
Wharf Vw MK18 3 C3
Wharfside MK2 30 C4
Wharfside Pl MK18 3 C3
Wheatcroft Cl MK6 23 G6
Wheatfield Cl LU7 39 H2
Wheatley Cl MK4 28 C3
Wheelers La MK13 16 A2
Wheelwrights Mews MK14 17 F2
Wheelwrights Way MK19 9 E5
Whetstone Cl MK13 16 B5
Whichford MK14 13 G6
Whitby Cl MK3 29 F3
White Alder MK12 11 G6
White Horse Dr MK4 28 C3
White House Ct LU7 39 E3
Whitebaker Ct MK14 17 F3
Whitegate Ct MK6 23 H4
Whitehall Av MK10 25 G2
Whitehorse Yd MK11 10 A6
Whiteley Cres MK3 33 E1
Whitethorns MK16 13 H3
Whitsun Pasture MK15 17 H2
Whitton Way MK16 13 H3
Whitworth La MK5 22 B3
Wickstead Av MK8 26 D1
Wildacre Rd MK5 22 A6
Wilford Cl MK15 24 A1
Wilkscroft MK5 22 A4
Willen La MK14 13 F6
Willen Park Av MK15 17 H2
Willen Rd MK16 14 A3
Willets Rise MK5 22 A5
Willey Ct MK11 20 B1
William Smith Cl MK15 18 A5
William Sutton Ho MK5 22 B4
Williams Circle MK7 25 E6
Williams Cl MK19 7 B1
Willow Bank Walk LU7 39 G2
Willow Cl MK16 15 H6
Willow Dr MK18 3 D5
Willow Gro MK19 9 E5
Willow Ho, Leighton Buzzard LU7 38 C3
Willow Ho, Milton Keynes MK14 16 C3
Willow La MK11 9 F6
Willow Way MK2 30 A6
Willow Wren MK14 13 E5
Willowford MK13 11 H6
Wilmin Gro MK5 22 B4
Wilsley Pound MK7 25 E2
Wilson Ct MK8 26 E1
Wilton Av MK3 29 G5
Wiltshire Way MK3 29 E3
Wimbledon Pl MK13 4 B1
Wimborne Cres MK4 27 F5
Wincanton Hill MK3 28 C6
Winchester Circle MK10 25 F1
Windermere Dr MK2 34 A2
Windermere Gdns LU7 38 A3
Windmill Cl MK18 3 D3
Windmill Hill Dr MK3 28 C6
Windrush Cl MK15 17 G2
Windsor Av, Leighton Buzzard LU7 38 D2
Windsor Av, Newport Pagnell MK16 14 A2
Windsor St, Fenny Stratford MK2 30 A5
Windsor St, Wolverton MK12 11 F5
Winemar Cl MK19 7 C1
Winfold La MK4 28 B4
Wing Rd LU7 38 A6
Wingate Circle MK7 31 E1
Wingfield Gro MK10 25 E1
Winsford Hill MK4 29 E2
Winstanley La MK5 28 C1
Winston Cl LU7 39 E1
Winterburn MK13 16 B4
Winwood Cl MK19 9 B7
Wisewood Rd MK5 26 E3
Wishart Grn MK7 25 H6
Wisley Av MK13 4 C1
Wistmans MK4 28 D1
Witan Ct MK9 4 C4
Witan Gate MK9 4 C3
Witan Gate Ho MK9 4 C4
Witham Ct MK3 28 D4
Withington MK13 16 B3
Withycombe MK4 29 E2
Wittmills Oak MK18 3 C3
Woad La MK14 13 E6
Woburn Av MK12 11 E6
Woburn Ct LU7 38 C3
Woburn La MK17 36 E2
Woburn Pl LU7 37 C6
Woburn Rd, Leighton Buzzard LU7 37 C2
Woburn Rd, Little Brickhill MK17 35 H1
Woburn Rd, Woburn Sands MK17 36 C3
Woburn Sands Rd MK17 31 G3
Wolfscote La MK4 28 B2
Wolsey Gdns MK13 16 A4
Wolston Mdw MK10 18 C6
Wolverton Rd, Castlethorpe MK19 6 C2
Wolverton Rd, Great Linford MK14 12 C6
Wolverton Rd, Haversham MK19 11 G1
Wolverton Rd, Newport Pagnell MK16 13 G3
Wolverton Rd, Stony Stratford MK11 10 A6
Wolverton Rd, Wolverton MK19 11 G3
Wood End La MK16 15 H6
Wood La, Aspley Guise MK17 36 D3
Wood La, Great Linford MK14 17 E1
Wood St, New Bradwell MK13 11 H4
Wood St, Woburn Sands MK17 36 B2
Woodhouse Ct MK14 16 C2
Woodland Av LU7 37 B6
Woodland Cl LU7 37 C2
Woodland Vw MK12 11 F6
Woodland Way MK17 36 B3
Woodlands Cl MK18 3 C2
Woodlands Cres MK18 3 B2
Woodley Headland MK6 23 H4
Woodman Cl LU7 39 F3
Woodmans Cl MK19 9 B7
Woodruff Av MK14 17 E5
Woodrush Cl MK6 29 G1
Woods La NN12 8 A1
Woodside, Aspley Guise MK17 36 D3
Woodside, Stony Stratford MK11 10 B6
Woodside Way LU7 38 C4
Woodspring Ct MK10 24 D2
Woodstock Ct MK13 16 B1
Woodville Cres NN12 6 B5
Woodward Pl MK8 22 A1
Woolrich Gdns MK11 20 A1
Worcester Cl MK16 13 F3
Wordsworth Av MK16 13 F2
Wordsworth Dr MK3 29 F6
Worrelle Av MK10 18 D5
Worth Ct MK10 25 E2
Wray Ct MK4 28 B3
Wren Cl MK18 3 D5
Wrens Pk MK10 19 E6
Wroxton Ct MK4 27 F5
Wyblington Dr MK6 29 G1
Wye Cl MK3 29 E4
Wylie End MK13 16 A2
Wymondham MK10 25 E1
Wyness Av MK17 35 H2
Wyngates LU7 38 C4
Wynyard Ct MK6 23 E3

Xscape Entertainment Centre MK9 5 H3

Yalts Brow MK4 28 B3
Yardley Ct NN12 6 B4
Yardley Rd, Cosgrove MK19 8 F2
Yardley Rd, Milton Keynes MK19 10 A1
Yardley Rd, Potterspury NN12 8 B1
Yardley Rd, Towcester NN12 6 C6
Yarrow Pl MK14 17 E4
Yeats Cl MK16 13 F2
Yeomans Dr MK14 13 G6
Yew Tree Cl MK17 32 C4
Yew Tree Ct, Leighton Buzzard LU7 39 E2
Yew Tree Ct, Milton Keynes MK19 7 C2
Yonder Slade MK18 3 C6
York Ct LU7 38 D2
York Ho MK3 29 E5
York Rd MK11 9 F6
Youngs Ind Est LU7 39 H3

PLEASE NOTE: No part of this publication may be reproduced, stored in a retrieval system or transmitted in any format or by any means, electronic, mechanical, photocopying, recording or otherwise, without the prior permission of Red Books (Estate Publications) Ltd and Ordnance Survey.

POSTCODES have been reproduced with the permission of The Post Office. Every care has been taken by Red Books (Estate Publications) Ltd but The Post Office cannot be held responsible for any errors or omissions. The outward part of the Postcode which is reproduced in this index will not suffice in identifying a particular address. The list of Postcodes is a copyright work of The Post Office.

Red Books showing the way

For the latest publication list, prices and to order online please visit our website

LOCAL STREET ATLASES

Abingdon, Didcot
Aldershot, Camberley
Alfreton, Belper
Andover
Ashford, Tenterden
Aylesbury, Tring
Bangor, Caernarfon
Barnstaple, Bideford
Basildon, Billericay
Basingstoke, Alton
Bath, Bradford-on-Avon
Bedford
Bodmin, Wadebridge
Bournemouth
Bracknell
Brentwood
Brighton
Bristol
Bromley
Burton upon Trent
Bury Saint Edmunds, Stowmarket
Cambridge
Cannock, Rugeley
Cardiff
Carlisle, Penrith
Chelmsford, Braintree
Chester, Wrexham
Chesterfield, Dronfield
Chichester, Bognor Regis
Chippenham, Calne
Coatbridge, Airdrie
Colchester, Clacton-on-Sea
Corby, Kettering, Wellingborough
Coventry, Rugby
Crawley, Mid-Sussex
Crewe, Nantwich
Derby
Dundee, Saint Andrews
Eastbourne, Hailsham
Edinburgh
Exeter, Exmouth
Falkirk, Grangemouth
Fareham, Gosport
Flintshire Towns
Folkestone, Dover
Glasgow
Gloucester, Cheltenham
Gravesend, Dartford
Grays, Thurrock
Great Yarmouth, Lowestoft
Grimsby, Cleethorpes
Guildford, Woking
Hamilton, Motherwell
Harlow, Bishops Stortford
Harrogate, Knaresborough
Hastings, Bexhill
Hereford
Hertford, Waltham Cross
High Wycombe
Huntingdon, Saint Neots
Ipswich
Isle of Man
Isle of Wight
Kendal, Windermere
Kidderminster, Stourport-on-Severn
Kingston upon Hull
Lancaster, Morecambe
Leicester
Lincoln, Washingborough
Llandudno, Colwyn Bay
Loughborough, Coalville
Luton, Dunstable
Macclesfield, Wilmslow
Maidstone
Mansfield, Sutton in Ashfield
Medway, Gillingham
Mid Wales Towns
Milton Keynes
New Forest
Newark-on-Trent
Newbury, Thatcham
Newport, Chepstow
Newquay, Perranporth
Northampton
Northwich, Winsford
Norwich

Nottingham
Nuneaton, Bedworth
Oxford, Kidlington
Penzance, Saint Ives
Perth, Kinross
Peterborough, Stamford
Plymouth
Portsmouth
Reading, Henley-on-Thames
Redditch, Kidderminster
Reigate, Mole Valley
Rhyl, Prestatyn
Rugby
Saint Albans, Welwyn, Hatfield
Saint Austell, Lostwithiel
Salisbury, Wilton
Scarborough, Whitby
Scunthorpe
Sevenoaks
Shrewsbury
Sittingbourne, Faversham
Slough, Maidenhead, Windsor
Solihull
Southampton
Southend-on-Sea
Stafford
Stevenage, Letchworth
Stirling, Alloa
Stoke-on-Trent
Stroud, Nailsworth
Swansea
Swindon, Chippenham
Tamworth, Lichfield
Taunton, Bridgwater
Telford, Newport
Tenby, Saundersfoot
Thanet, Canterbury
Torbay, Newton Abbot
Trowbridge, Frome
Truro, Falmouth
Tunbridge Wells, Tonbridge
Walsall
Warwick, Royal Leamington Spa
Watford, Hemel Hempstead
Wells, Glastonbury
West Midlands, Birmingham
Weston-super-Mare
Weymouth, Dorchester
Winchester
Worcester
Workington, Whitehaven
Worthing, Littlehampton
Wrexham
York

COUNTY STREET ATLASES
(Town Centre Maps)
Bedfordshire
Berkshire
Buckinghamshire
Cambridgeshire
Cheshire
Cornwall
Cumbria
Derbyshire
Devon
Dorset
East Sussex
Essex
Gloucestershire
Hampshire
Herefordshire
Hertfordshire
Kent
Leicestershire, Rutland
Lincolnshire
Norfolk
Northamptonshire
Nottinghamshire
Oxfordshire
Shropshire
Somerset
Staffordshire
Suffolk
Surrey
Warwickshire
West Sussex

Wiltshire
Worcestershire

EUROPEAN STREET MAPS
Calais & Boulogne Shoppers Map (Sheet Map)
Dieppe Shoppers Map (Sheet Map)
North French Towns Street Atlas

LEISURE & TOURIST MAPS
Argyll & The Isles
Argyll, The Isles, Loch Lomond, Stirling & Trossachs
British Isles
Caithness & Sutherland
Chilterns & Thames Valley
Cornwall
Cotswolds & Severn Valley
Dartmoor & South Devon Coast
Devon
Devon & Cornwall
Dorset & The Channel Islands
East Anglia
Edinburgh & The Lothians
England & Wales
Exmoor & North Devon Coast
Fife (Kingdom of)
Fort William, Ben Nevis & Glen Coe
Grampian Highlands & Aberdeen
Great Britain
Greater Glasgow & Clyde Valley
Greater London (M25)
Heart of Scotland
Highlands of Scotland
Historic Scotland
Iona & Mull
Isle of Arran
Isle of Man
Isle of Man (Deluxe)
Isle of Wight
Kent & East Sussex
Kent to Cornwall
Lake District
Loch Lomond
Loch Ness & Aviemore
North Pennines & Lakes
North West England
North York Moors
Orkney & Shetland Islands
Outer Hebrides
Peak District
Perthshire
Scotland
Scotland (Atlas)
Scotland (Homelands of the Clans)
Shetland & Orkney Islands
Skye & Lochalsh
Snowdonia
South East England
South East England
Southern England
Surrey & Sussex Downs
Sussex
The Cotswolds
The Mid Shires
The Shires of Middle England
Wales
Wales (Atlas)
Wessex
Yorkshire
Yorkshire Dales

EUROPEAN LEISURE MAPS
Belgium, Luxembourg & Netherlands
Cross Channel Visitors Map
Europe
France & Belgium
Germany
Ireland
Italy
Spain & Portugal

WORLD MAPS
World Map - Political
World Travel Adventure Map

RED BOOKS (ESTATE PUBLICATIONS) Ltd, Bridewell House, Tenterden, Kent. TN30 6EP
Tel: 01580 764225   Fax: 01580 763720   Email: sales@redbooks-maps.co.uk